at 714.

## Rally to Precede
## Opening of Bible
## Institute Course

In preparation for the opening of
the new Reformed Bible institute,
a public rally will be held at 8
o'clock Wednesday evening at the
Sherman Street Christian Reformed church. Officers and board
members of the institution will ex-

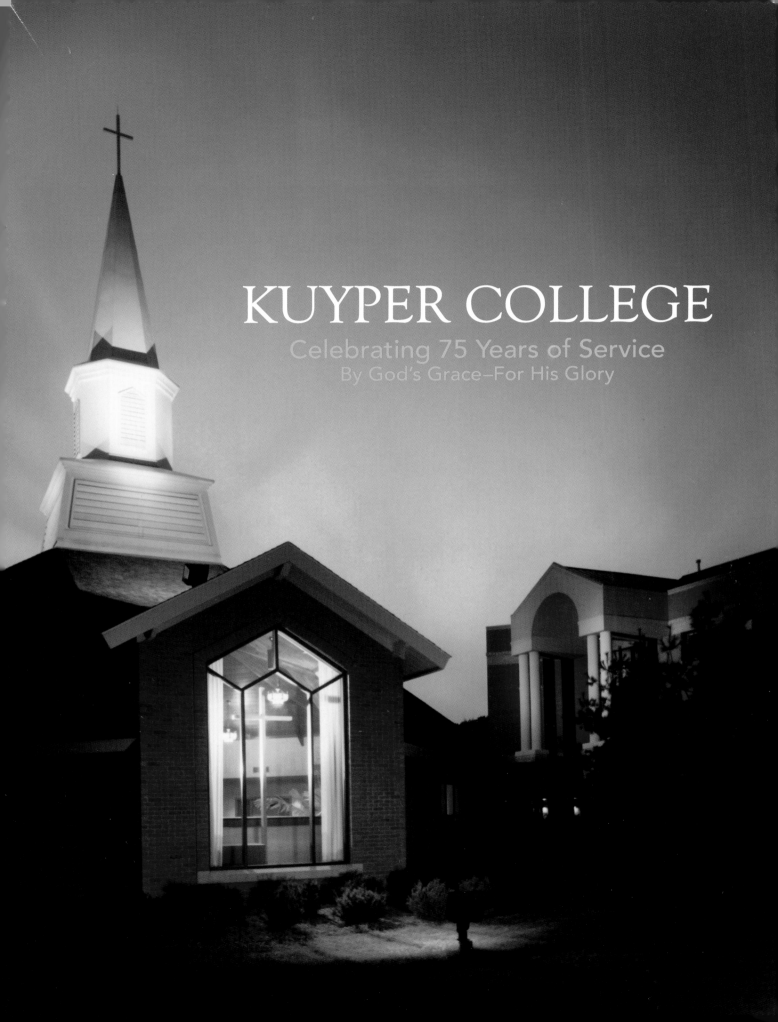

# KUYPER COLLEGE

### Celebrating 75 Years of Service
By God's Grace—For His Glory

# KUYPER COLLEGE

## Celebrating 75 Years of Service
### By God's Grace—For His Glory

*by Anne Bauman and Dr. Paul Bremer*

The Donning Company Publishers
184 Business Park Drive, Suite 206
Virginia Beach, VA 23462

Steve Mull, General Manager
Barbara Buchanan, Office Manager
Anne Burns, Editor
Rick Boley, Graphic Designer
Kathy Adams, Imaging Artist
Sherry Hartman, Project Research Coordinator
Nathan Stufflebean, Research and Marketing
    Supervisor
Steve Hartman, Project Director

Cataloging-in-Publication Data available from the Library of Congress

ISBN 978-1-57864-888-7

Printed in the United States of America at Walsworth Publishing Company

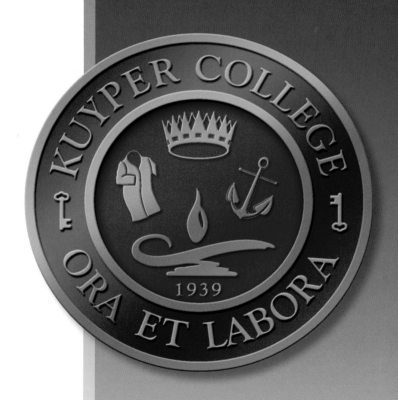

THE
DONNING COMPANY
PUBLISHERS

# Table of Contents

# Foreword

How do you summarize seventy-five years of the life an institution? That is a challenge in preparing a book such as this.

The life of an institution involves people who had a vision for founding it, people who were willing to support a fledgling institution with little assurance of its survival, and people who shaped its mission and guided it when it faced significant challenges and difficulties.

The story of this organization involves the grace of God and the diligent effort of many people who served it. We regret we have not been able to mention all the people who served the organization over the years. Paraphrasing a line in Hebrews 11:32, we remember that "time would fail us to tell of" all of them.

These people include faculty and board of trustee members; personnel in the business office, library, and development office; maintenance and secretarial staffs; food service employees; and numerous others. Each one of them made a significant contribution to the work and success of the college.

In the early 1900s a number of individuals recognized the need for a training program in Bible and evangelism to equip people who were unable to go to seminary. They could then increase their knowledge of the Bible and witness in the communities where they lived, in other areas of the United States, and throughout the world.

A number of board members from Grand Rapids and Chicago formed the Reformed Bible Institute (RBI) even after the Synod of the Christian Reformed Church was unwilling initially to support such an endeavor. Rev. Henry J. Kuiper, editor of *The Banner* of the Christian Reformed Church, played a key role as a member of the founding board and faithfully served as its president until his death.

RBI did not have an established location. Its first home was in the upstairs of a building on Wealthy Street. As time went on the institute bought other properties and finally purchased a home with a number of landscaped acres adjoining it at 1869 Robinson Road. As the institution grew, its supporters enlarged the campus on Robinson Road, increased its curricular offerings, and helped it become a four-year college recognized by the State of Michigan and two accrediting bodies. Later it sold its campus to its neighbor, Aquinas College, and built a new campus along the East Beltline in northeast Grand Rapids.

Without God's grace and the diligent work of numerous individuals, the institution would not have survived and flourished. This document is a tribute to these individuals and the story of what developed as their vision came to fruition.

—Dr. Paul Bremer

## Chapter 1

# The Roots of the Reformed Bible Institute

Over the last seventy-five years, it has been abundantly clear that God has been the one orchestrating the foundation and growth of the Reformed Bible Institute into what it is today. From a few people with a vision and a handful of students studying in a cramped room above a cafe, Kuyper College is now a respected educational institution with graduates serving the Lord around the world.

Through all of the growing pains during the school's early years, one thing is clear: the purpose and mission of the original founders is still shared by the school's leadership today. The focus is and always has been equipping people to serve the Lord and seek His will—whether that is in a remote missionary location, in the business world, in a local church, or in any other location we His children serve.

By God's grace, Kuyper College exists—for His glory.

By God's grace, a need was felt for Christian education for laypeople and a qualified, passionate group of people paved the way. By God's grace, the school found a person to popularize the idea of a new school and give leadership to it. By God's grace, the institute located a place to begin its operation and found new spaces to carry on its work as it expanded. By God's grace, the school had competent faculty members that guided students through their study of the Bible. By God's grace, students came to be taught to serve others—all to the glory of Him.

Praise be to God.

## Early Ties to the Christian Reformed Church

Though the Reformed Bible Institute was not specifically affiliated with the Christian Reformed Church (CRC), early supporters and founders maintained close ties to that denomination. When examining the roots of the Reformed Bible Institute, it is helpful to look at the Christian Reformed Church and the mission movement within that denomination in the late 1800s and early 1900s.

During that time, many of the members of the Christian Reformed Church were recent immigrants from the Netherlands. They faced challenges in adjusting to a new land and a new culture. Most of their conversations and religious documents were in the Dutch language. That limited their interest and ability in sharing the gospel with others in the new land in which they settled.

Slowly they gained a larger perspective. In 1889, the first CRC missionary was installed and began work among the Sioux Indians on Rosebud Agency, Dakota Territory, but the work was abandoned within a year. Denominational outreach began among the Navajo people in 1896 in New Mexico and among the Zuni people of New Mexico in 1897.

Apart from these instances, mission work sponsored by the CRC was not a prominent feature of the denomination. According to

Hoezee and Meehan in their book *Flourishing in the Land* which describes the missionary effort of the CRC, "While many of the churches in America were busy recruiting missionaries, the CRC seemed largely content to do self-maintenance...The simple fact is that many in the early days of the CRC appeared more interested in maintaining their Dutch ethnicity and staunch doctrines than in reaching out to those beyond their kin." Though many other Christian denominations in the United States were engaging wholeheartedly into mission work in the early part of the twentieth century, the Christian Reformed Church lagged behind.

In 1920, Johanna Veenstra, a single woman and member of the Christian Reformed Church, began working in Nigeria with the Sudan United Mission, a British missionary organization. Before her departure, Veenstra wrote an article published in *The Banner*, the CRC's newly created periodical. In her article, Veenstra detailed the need and her desire for a missionary training school that would also train church members in Bible knowledge and work in missionary outreach. She knew women would be able to assist the church in its work and suggested

Johanna Veenstra, a single woman and member of the Christian Reformed Church, began working as a missionary in Nigeria in 1920. Before she began mission work, she wrote an article on the need for a missionary training school that was published in *The Banner*. Source: *Pioneering for Christ in the Sudan* by Johanna Veenstra, Smitter Book Company, 1926.

a new educational organization could train both men and women for evangelism and missions according to Reformed theological principles. "Very often I receive a letter from or meet personally some young person, who wishes to take up some definite training, but who is at a loss to know which way to turn to secure that training," noted Veenstra.

Locally, while there was rapid growth of city missions in Grand Rapids from 1918 to 1939 due to consecrated laymen and a vocal minority among the clergy, there were little other early focused, documented efforts to enter into and encourage domestic evangelization. Dr. Dick L. Van Halsema, the president of Reformed Bible College (RBC) from 1966 to 1987, later posited that until 1926, "there was no report of denominational activity among unchurched Americans."

After 1926, several proposals were presented to the CRC Synod (the annual meeting for the denomination) for training courses in evangelism for laypeople. In 1930, a request was presented for a synodically approved training program for young missionary enthusiasts due to concern that Christian Reformed students who studied at Moody Bible Institute in Chicago would not continue work in the CRC denomination upon graduation.

In 1932, Synod appointed a committee "to consider the advisability and feasibility of establishing a Training School for lay evangelistic workers" and it was recommended mission courses be established at Calvin Seminary. The seminary was formed to prepare ordained pastors, but the vision of training lay evangelistic workers was not a part of its purpose. However, a leadership training school was established at Calvin Seminary after the Synod of 1934 but was discontinued by 1936 due to a lack of sufficient enrollment.

But by 1936, attitudes were beginning to change in the Christian Reformed Church about the need for domestic missions, and in 1937, groups in the church made the appeal for evangelistic work to Synod. The 1937 Synod called for a report to explore the possibility of a "complete program and budget for a real Missionary Training and Bible School." An elaborate Bible school program was submitted to Synod in 1938 with an annual cost of $25,000, but once again, this proposed Bible school was not approved by Synod.

## H. J. Kuiper's Passion for Community Evangelism

In 1912, the pastor of Prospect Park Christian Reformed Church in Holland, Michigan, Rev. H. J. Kuiper, who would later serve as the president of the board of the Reformed Bible Institute, approached the church's consistory with a request: to find someone to work alongside him in that congregation and to coordinate an evangelistic outreach in Holland. But no training school existed in Reformed circles for such a need. Where would such a worker be found?

Despite the lack of formal evangelistic training, John Van De Water was appointed to that position, and together he and Kuiper established a city mission endeavor in Holland. Kuiper left Prospect Park in 1913 to assume the pastorate at Second Englewood Church in Chicago and persuaded Van De Water to follow him there so they could continue mission work. Upon their arrival, Kuiper and Van De Water discovered several Chicago-area churches were already involved in a sort of "missions training school" at the Helping Hand Mission, near downtown. For the next five years, Kuiper and Van De Water closely observed the functions of the mission as they served their own congregation in the Chicago area.

Back in Grand Rapids in 1928, volunteer mission workers felt more city mission work needed to be done, so they approached local ministers. To address the issue, a board for the mission was established, and H. J. Kuiper, who had moved from Chicago to Grand Rapids that year to serve as pastor of Broadway Christian Reformed Church, was appointed as its leader. The board proceeded to call John Van De Water, who came to serve as a city missionary, and on Easter Sunday 1929, the West Fulton Street Mission opened as a result of their efforts.

Many years later, Kuiper reflected on the difficulty he faced in finding a teacher and helper to work alongside him during the early part of the twentieth century. Other Reformed schools, such as the Theological School (now Calvin Theological Seminary), focused on training pastors, but the curriculum was not designed to educate teachers, church lay workers, or evangelists. John Calvin Junior College (now Calvin College) was designed as a feeder for the seminary and provided four years of high school and two years of college. There was a definite gap in the training of young people to be church planters and lay evangelists—another school was needed.

Henry J. Kuiper was the editor of *The Banner*, the Christian Reformed Church's official magazine from 1929 to 1956. Kuiper was one of the founders of the RBI and served as the chairman of the board until his death in 1962.

John Van De Water worked with H. J. Kuiper for many years beginning in 1913 at Prospect Park Christian Reformed Church in Holland, Michigan. In 1929, Van De Water and Kuiper would begin the West Fulton Street Mission in Grand Rapids. Source: *Harvest of Hearts* by John Van De Water, Zondervan, 1953.

## The Chicago Roots of the Reformed Bible Institute

During the time classes were conducted at the Chicago Helping Hand Mission, evening classes were also taking place in Cicero and the Roseland areas of Chicago. The lay leaders of these classes were often enrolled at Moody Bible Institute to receive some sort of Christian education, though the Christian Reformed Church would have preferred training that taught Reformed principles of theology. But with the onset of the Great Depression, interest and resources for these Chicago classes waned and were discontinued, and the matter was dropped.

Before classes ended, Chicago-area churches petitioned the Christian Reformed Church in 1928 for its support and approval to expand the evening classes into a day school. However, the petition to Synod did not surface until 1936, when it was decided it would be too expensive of an endeavor for the amount of demonstrated interest. At that time, Synod also did not recommend placing these specialized courses in evangelism and missions into the permanent curriculum at what was coming to be known as Calvin College and Seminary.

Despite the lack of support, Rev. George Weeber, the superintendent of the Chicago Helping Hand Mission, and Mark Fakkema, executive secretary of the National

You are Invited to Attend

**The Evening Courses**
*given by the*
**Reformed Bible Institute of Chicago**

Christ ... our Life. Col.3.4 | Life Light of men Joh.1.4

The Institute has been reorganized. It now is operated under a Board appointed by consistories of the Christian Reformed Church. It is to be known as the Reformed Bible Institute of Chicago.

The present South Side and West Side branches will continue as heretofore. New students, however, may enroll with the new term beginning January 5, 1940.

Beginning with the new term a number of new courses will be offered in a central location (Englewood). This will give students from all sections an added opportunity of study and fellowship.

The Bible institute movement was not limited to west Michigan and had strong roots in Chicago, where a Reformed Bible institute continued into the 1940s. The Chicago RBI offered classes (primarily evening classes) in two different locations in the '30s and '40s.

Mark Fakkema was instrumental in starting a Bible school in Chicago and was one of the founding board members of the Reformed Bible Institute in Grand Rapids.

Union of Christian Schools (now Christian Schools International), met in Chicago to discuss Weeber's dream of a Reformed Bible school in the spring of 1936. "[Fakkema's] response was immediate and enthusiastic in that he also had had the same idea in mind for some time," recalled Weeber. "We then and there made plans as to the proper procedure to realize our mutual aspiration."

It was agreed that it was most fitting and practical to establish such a school under the auspices of the Chicago Helping Hand Mission. The idea for the establishment of a Reformed Bible institute was presented to the mission board and to the five supporting consistories, all of whom readily approved and endorsed the idea.

From there, plans moved ahead quickly to begin the new school. An educational committee was created. Two instructors were appointed—Weeber and Fakkema—who willingly volunteered to serve without pay. The committee decided to hold evening classes in the South Side Christian School at 108th and Princeton, Roseland, and in the West Side Christian School at 14th Street and 59th Avenue, Cicero, and the name "The Reformed Bible Institute" was chosen.

The response was immediate and gratifying, and two summer and two winter terms were held. The first summer term ran from May 27 to July 26, 1937, at both locations. More than one hundred students participated and were not charged tuition, though a free-will offering took place during each session. Enrollment swelled to two hundred by 1938, and talk began that a regular day school should be established.

In the spring of 1938, the educational committee in charge of the classes in Chicago approached the CRC Classis of Illinois to take charge of the school. Recognizing the potential national impact the school could have, Classis Illinois recommended the committee take their proposal to the Christian Reformed Church Synod, which they did. In its reply, Synod stated it was "delighted" with the local work done and it "heartily" recommended this work "for intercession, attendance, and financial support." However, Synod ultimately decided not to take over the project, leaving it in the hands of those at the local level.

## REFORMED BIBLE INSTITUTE
*"In thy light shall we see light"*—Ps. 36.9.

# What Students Say

The Reformed Bible Institute is a school for training of young people and adults in *Self-development* and in *Christian Service*.

The Institute comprises two Branches: SOUTH SIDE—Roseland Christian School (108th Street and Princeton Avenue); WEST SIDE — Timothy Christian School (corner 14th Street and 59th Avenue).

*Monday* evening is "Institute Night" at the West Side Branch. *Monday* and *Wednesday* evenings are the "Institute Nights" for the South Side Branch.

*Under the Auspices of*
**CHICAGO HELPING HAND MISSION**
1938
CHICAGO, ILLINOIS

This pamphlet advertised the evening classes of the Reformed Bible Institute in Chicago in 1938.

**Reformed Bible Institute**
Under Auspices of CHICAGO HELPING HAND MISSION
**Certificate of Credit**

This certifies that *John Fennema*
has successfully completed the work of the *Fall*
Term ( *seven* 45 min. periods) in the subject of
*Introductory Bible*
*Mark Fakkema* Principal
*N. Youngsma* Pres. of Board
Date *Jan 8, 1938*

This certificate verifies that a student successfully completed the fall 1937 term of seven, forty-five-minute class periods of the Reformed Bible Institute of Chicago. Mark Fakkema, who was the principal of the school at the time, played a large role in helping to begin the RBI in Grand Rapids.

# CHRISTIAN REFORMED PUBLISHING HOUSE

**The Banner**
WEEKLY PAPER OF CHRISTIAN REFORMED CHURCH
H. J. KUIPER, EDITOR

**De Wachter**
PUBLISHED WEEKLY --- HOLLAND LANGUAGE
H. KEEGSTRA, EDITOR

ALSO PUBLISHERS OF SUNDAY SCHOOL PAPERS, PSALTER HYMNAL, AND YEARBOOK
J. J. BUITEN, Business Manager
52 MARKET AVE., NW., GRAND RAPIDS, MICH.

November 10, 1937.

Mr. George J. Stob,
1512 South 57th Ave.,
Cicero, Illinois.

Dear Brother:

The announcement you sent me to The
Banner will be placed. I have no objections
whatsoever. As a matter of fact, I think
Chicago is a good place for the establishment of such a Bible institute. I like
its emphasis on being Reformed. Some day
our church is going to have a full-fledged
Bible institute, unless I am badly mistaken.

If your school gets the right start,
you will be several jumps ahead of any other
locality, although I see several advantages
in having such a school in Grand Rapids. At
all events, I wish you success.

There are two or three things which I
like to stress, if I may. First, be very
careful about the personnel of your teaching
staff! Think of the Chicago Christian High
School. Second, keep the school with the
church as an institute. I believe that is
far safer. Third, try to make it a day school
just as soon as you can. It seems to me experience tends to show that all these evening
schools peter out in time.

I want to thank you for your suggestion
in regard to a bull's eye corner. I shall
think it over and talk it over with our edi-
torial committee when we get together in the
near future to make plans for our Young People's
Department.

Yours very sincerely,

H. J. Kuiper

HJK:DG

This letter from H. J. Kuiper to George J. Stob dated November 10, 1937, encouraged Stob's Bible institute endeavors in Chicago. Both would later be members of the founding board of the Reformed Bible Institute.

## Opposition to the Reformed Bible Institute

As discussions continued and interest swelled for the proposed school, several arguments against the school were voiced. Much of the discussion occurred in *The Banner* in the late 1930s where Rev. H. J. Kuiper had been exploring and encouraging the idea of a school through numerous articles. Along with Kuiper's articles of support for the school, *The Banner* also published several articles and letters from individuals voicing their concerns.

One of the biggest concerns against the school was simply that the CRC Synod did not support it. Similarly, the Chicago day school during the 1930s was not supported by the CRC and was not even supported by the five consistories that oversaw the Chicago Helping Hand Mission.

Another concern some people voiced was that the proposed Bible school would serve as a "shortcut" to ordained ministry. The school's mission was to prepare laypeople for lives of service, but it was clearly stated from the beginning that if students wanted to go into ordained ministry, they would have to get further education at a seminary of their choice. Supporters of the school understood the demands for biblical education were increasing among laypeople and there was a real need for evangelists and mission workers who would not be able to attend seminary.

After the school was established and had been operating for several semesters, Johanna Timmer, the first instructor of the Reformed Bible Institute, addressed this persistent concern in the April 1942 *RBI Quarterly*. "We do not, we positively do not, exist to offer a short-cut to the Christian ministry...I, for one, would not be satisfied with a minister whose professional training was limited to

what the RBI offers," Timmer stressed. Dr. John C. DeKorne, a founding board member, also wrote in the Vol. 2 No. 2 *RBI Quarterly* that "neither its entrance requirements, nor its avowed purpose, nor its course of instructions would permit it to train young men for the ministry of the Gospel" in a pastoral setting.

One of the lesser but more humorous concerns voiced was there was no need for a school because people wondered whether there was a similar school back in the Netherlands. If the church "back home" didn't need a school for laypeople, why did the church here need one? Other points noted were the concern there would not be enough positions for graduates within the Christian Reformed denomination and the school would lower the high standard of education the CRC had held to through Calvin College and Seminary.

Over time, it became evident there was indeed a need for a school to train laypeople and RBI would do so in a manner consistent with biblical teaching and the Christian Reformed Church's theological concerns. RBI was not formed to train pastors but was formed to teach men and women about the Bible and instill a passion for evangelism and mission work, and that is what it did.

Dr. John C. DeKorne was the director of mission for the Christian Reformed Church from 1939 to 1951 and served as the vice president of the founding board.

# The Founding Board of the
# Reformed Bible Institute

**The founding fourteen board members in 1939 included both men and women:**

- Dr. John C. DeKorne (1888–1951): Director of Missions for the CRC from 1939 to 1951
- Mr. Mark Fakkema (1890–1970): Executive Secretary of National Union of Christian Schools (now Christian Schools International)
- Dr. Oren Holtrop (1898–2000): Pastor of East Side Christian Reformed Church in Cleveland, Ohio
- Rev. H. J. Kuiper (1885–1962): Pastor of Neland Avenue Christian Reformed Church in Grand Rapids and Editor of *The Banner* from 1928 to 1956
- Mr. Albert Reitsma: Chicago-area (Oak Park) businessman
- Rev. John H. Schaal (1908–2002): Pastor of Milwood Christian Reformed Church in Kalamazoo, Michigan
- Rev. Cornelius Schoolland (1898–1985): Pastor of Harderwyk Christian Reformed Church in Holland, Michigan
- Mr. George J. Stob (1902–1958): Chicago-area (Cicero) businessman

- Miss Johanna Timmer (1901–1978): Dean of Women at Calvin College
- *Rev. John Vander Ploeg (1902–1983): Pastor of East Paris Christian Reformed Church in Grand Rapids
- Mr. G. B. Van Heyningen: Chicago businessman
- Rev. William Van Peursem (1901–1999): Pastor of Sherman Street Christian Reformed Church in Grand Rapids
- Miss Agnes Vellenga (1904–1995): Former teacher at Racine Christian School (Wisconsin); served as a missionary in Paterson, New Jersey, as a member of Paterson's Madison Avenue Christian Reformed Church, from 1941 to 1949; served as a missionary in Manila, Philippines, as a member of Third Reformed Church in Grand Rapids, from 1955 to 1977
- *Mr. P. J. Zondervan (1909–1993): Co-founder of Zondervan® Publishers in Grand Rapids

\* Absent from the March 28 meeting but added later

Several members of the founding board of the Reformed Bible Institute were present on the first day of classes on January 4, 1940.

## Church Leaders Meet to Form the Reformed Bible Institute

During 1937 and 1938, Rev. H. J. Kuiper and Rev. William Van Peursem, pastor of Sherman Street Christian Reformed Church in Grand Rapids, conducted a series of exploratory meetings. Despite some opposition, they felt the time had come to begin a day school. Kuiper, then the pastor of Neland Avenue Christian Reformed Church, invited a group of people who shared the vision to a meeting in his Grand Rapids home, the parsonage of Neland CRC, on March 28, 1939.

This group covenanted together to begin a day school to "fill the thus far neglected gap in our educational program." Kuiper was elected the first chairman of the board of trustees, a capacity in which he continued to serve until his death on December 12, 1962.

William Van Peursem was the pastor of Sherman Street Christian Reformed Church in Grand Rapids. He was one of the school's original board members and was one of the first three teachers at the Reformed Bible Institute.

A. S. De JONG, President
10554 Wentworth Ave., Chicago, Ill.

G. HEYNS, Vice-President
Holland, Mich.

HENRY KUIPER, Recording Secretary
1816 N. 3rd St., Sheboygan, Wis.

A. MEETER, Treasurer
Lansing, Ill.

## NATIONAL UNION OF CHRISTIAN SCHOOLS

MARK FAKKEMA, General Secretary
10119 Lafayette Avenue
CHICAGO, ILLINOIS

Jan. 20, 1939

Rev. C.M. Schoolland
R.R. 4
Holland, Mich.

Dear Brother:

Sorry you could not meet with us yesterday. May I render you a short report? The following persons were present: Rev. H.J. Kuiper, Rev. Van Peursem, Rev. Vander Ploeg, Dr. De Korne, Miss Timmer, Miss Vellenga, Mr. Zondervan, Mr. Geo. Stob and myself. Three decisions were informally agreed upon unanimously:

(1) We need a day school.
(2) That we begin an independent organization which would leave the door open to become an ecclesiastical institution at any time. For that reason we are for the time being to confine ourselves to the Chr. Ref. Church.
(3) That each one would send to undersigned some ideas which should go into the constitution of our society. We then are to draw up this constitution and submit it to the various members, after which we are to call another meeting. Please send us some of the things which should go into this constitution. Could you do that shortly?

The rest of the news I am sending you by way of a carbon copy mailed to Rev. Kuiper.

Cordially yours,

Mark

MF:CV

This note from Mark Fakkema to Rev. Cornelius Schoolland describes three decisions made at a January 19, 1939, meeting exploring the possibility of a school. A more official meeting establishing the Reformed Bible Institute would be held two months later, on March 28.

At that March 28 meeting, it was suggested by the four Chicago board members that fellow member Johanna Timmer become the field agent and instructor of the new school. "After Miss Timmer had left the room this proposal was duly discussed. The Board thereupon went on record to appoint Miss Timmer for part-time deputation work for the year beginning June 1, 1939, for the sum of $600.00—it being understood that as soon as developments permit Miss Timmer shall be given a teaching position in the Institute. It is

Johanna Timmer was the first acting head of the RBI and the first full-time faculty member. She is pictured here teaching in June 1940.

further understood that the members of this Board will underwrite the necessary money. In view of the money on hand each member agreed to underwrite the sum of $40.00," notes the minutes of the first official meeting of the board of the Reformed Bible Institute. Timmer agreed to the proposition and left her position as dean of women at Calvin College.

The board also decided no tuition would be charged and the RBI would do what it could to secure part-time employment for needy students to cover housing costs. If all went as planned, the institute would have dormitory space for both men and women, and room and board costs would be approximately $7.00 per week. To help cover costs, offerings would be taken at public meetings and conventions and at any other event held by the institute, and the school would accept donations from willing individuals and groups.

In another effort to raise support, the board formed the Reformed Bible Institute Association. Members would enroll for a $5.00 yearly fee that would help cover school costs. The association would choose a board to lead the institute and established four sub-committees: publicity, educational, building, and finance. A constitution was drafted with the association's purpose; guidelines for board members, faculty, and students of the institute; and theological basis for the association and institute.

Still to be determined was the question of location. At the June 12, 1939, board meeting (held at the 104th Street Christian School in Chicago), board members decided that Chicago would be an appropriate location for the new institute, provided a suitable location could be found. Chicago was an appropriate location, since evening classes were already being held there and were thriving.

## REGISTRATION AND TUITION

There is a registration fee of $10.00 payable in advance. This registration fee entitles acceptable students to the full three year course.

The Institute plans to operate without charging its students tuition.

## MEANS OF FINANCIAL SUPPORT

Article XII of the Constitution reads thus:

1. Regular membership dues are $5.00 per year.
2. Contributions are solicited from individuals or groups who would have a share in promoting the Kingdom cause represented by the Institute.
3. Offerings taken at public meetings, conventions, etc., held under the auspices of the Institute.
4. Since the Institute seeks primarily to fill a need in the Christian Reformed Church, it will solicit synodical cooperation for purposes of recommending this cause to the various congregations for moral and financial support.

## STUDENT HELP

The Reformed Bible Institute will do its utmost to secure part time employment for needy students.

## BOARD AND ROOM

At present Board and Room in Grand Rapids is charged at the rate of approximately $7.00 per week. If plans materialize the Institute will have dormitory facilities for both men and women.

## FOR FURTHER INFORMATION WRITE

The Rev. H. J. Kuiper, President
944 Neland Ave., Grand Rapids, Mich.

Dr. J. C. DeKorne, Vice-President
745 Benjamin Ave., Grand Rapids, Mich.

Mr. Mark Fakkema, Secretary
10119 Lafayette, Chicago, Illinois

Mr. George J. Stob, Treasurer
1512—57th Ave., Cicero, Illinois

Miss Johanna Timmer
619 Prince St., Grand Rapids, Mich.

This promotional pamphlet from 1939 details the costs of attending the institute and the ways the school planned to offset those costs.

The proposed course of study for students at the Reformed Bible Institute is detailed in this 1939 pamphlet. Knowledge of the Bible and the practical application of God's Word were heavily emphasized as they still are today.

## PROPOSED COURSE OF STUDY

1. A CLASSIFICATION OF COURSES TO BE TAUGHT
   A. THE BIBLE—ITS PLACE OF INFLUENCE
      1. Bible Introduction
      2. Religions of History
      3. A Study in Modernism
      4. Fundamentalism
      5. Current Denominations
      6. Anti-Christian Faiths
      7. Church History
      8. Foreign Missions
      9. Domestic Missions
      10. Christian Living
      11. The Biblical Principles of Missions
   B. THE BIBLE—ITS CONTENT
      1. Bible Geography
      2. Bible History
      3. The Pentateuch
      4. The Gospels
      5. Isaiah
      6. The Psalms
      7. Romans
      8. The Gospel of John
      9. Revelation
      10. The Unified Bible
      11. Bible Doctrine
      12. Bible Archeology
      13. Sunday School Lessons Explained
   C. THE BIBLE—METHODS OF PERSONAL EXPRESSION
      1. Personal Evangelism
      2. Public Speaking
      3. English
      4. Christian Leadership
      5. Practical Assignments
      6. Observation
      7. First Aid and Nursing

2. THE FOLLOWING COURSE OF STUDY ARRANGED FOR FIRST YEAR (3 TERMS)

FIRST TERM

Bible Introduction
The Gospels
Principles of Missions
Bible Doctrine
English
Bible History
Observation

The RBI Association was created as the school was being formed to raise funds and awareness for the school and to govern its existence.

Board member Mark Fakkema made his case for a Chicago location in *The Forward Look*, a 1940 report to the board of his observations. "The more our Institute grows the more it will be apparent that a Bible institute calls for a metropolitan environment... City missions will no doubt be the outstanding field of activity for our future graduates. While students they should be introduced to their future field of labor. As students they should become acquainted with prison work, hospital work, slum mission work, etc. In view of [current] world conditions (the impending WWII) foreign mission work may be largely confined to our own land," noted Fakkema.

But at the board meeting less than two months later held in Chicago on July 26, 1939, the group rescinded the motion regarding the Chicago location and decided to locate in Grand Rapids. Rev. William Van Peursem, another board member, recalled, "Some individuals had very touchy feelings on this question; however, I never sensed a feeling of anger. When the majority reached a decision, the others fell in line. I have always cherished that feeling of harmony." God was at work in the hearts and minds of each board member, and it was evident that His hand was divinely guiding the foundation of the fledgling institution.

## REFORMED BIBLE INSTITUTE

Grateful acknowledgement is made of the following contributions to the proposed Reformed Bible Institute:

A. G. Schaap, South Holland..........$ 5.00
Marion De Young, South Holland 10.00
Mrs. Harriet Haan, Highland............ 2.00
Cornelia Vis, Chicago........................ 5.00
Hattie Grevengoed, Oak Park.......... 5.00
Minnie Holtrust, Chicago.................. 10.00
John Holtrust, Chicago...................... 5.00
Margaret Pakkebier, Oak Park........ 10.00
Agnes Reitsma, Chicago.................... 10.00
Mark Fakkema, Chicago.................... 10.00
Rev. H. J. Kuiper, Grand Rapids... 10.00
P. J Zondervan, Grand Rapids...... 5.00
G. Evenhouse, Cicero........................ 20.00
G. J. Stob, Cicero.............................. 5.00

Johanna Timmer, Grand Rapids...... 10.00
Rev. Wm. Van Peursum, Grand
　Rapids............................................ 5.00
Simon Dekker, Chicago...................... 1.00
Willemetta Van Drunen, South
　Holland............................................ 5.00
Julius Tuene, Chicago........................ 5.00
Mrs. Grace Teune, Chicago.............. 5.00
Mrs. Grace Hoffman, Chicago.......... 5.00
Aldrich Evenhouse, Chicago............ 5.00
Richard Evenhouse, Cicero.............. 5.00
H. W. Groen, Denver.......................... 5.00
Dr. O. Holtrop, Cleveland................ 5.00
Peter Laning, Sr., Chicago................ 10.00
Garrett Laning, Chicago.................... 5.00
Albert Laning, Chicago...................... 5.00
Geraldine Laning, Chicago................ 2.00
Clarence Laning, Chicago.................. 5.00
W. Schipper, Chicago........................ 5.00
Rev. C. M. Schoolland, Holland...... 5.00

This article from *The Banner* (June 1, 1939) thanks those who contributed to the RBI. Several of the donors were members of the founding board.

committee recommended the annex of the 104th St. Christian School.

9. After considerable discussion a motion prevailed that we select Chicago as the location of our Institute provided a satisfactory location can be found.

10. The question of replying to some of the weightier arguments which were advanced was postponed until such a time when the definite location of the

At the June 12, 1939, board meeting, it was decided Chicago was the desired location for the Reformed Bible Institute to begin. However, less than two months later on July 26, the board rescinded that motion and decided to locate in Grand Rapids.

THE REFORMED
BIBLE INSTITUTE

ROOFING

MICHIGAN
HOME IMPROVEMENT CO.

The
REFORMED
BIBLE INSTITUTE

## Chapter 2

# Born in Faith, Nurtured in Prayer: 1939–1942

The founders of the Reformed Bible Institute were blessed from the beginning with a clear vision and sense of purpose. In a full-page informational article in the July/August 1939 issue of *The Young Calvinist,* the need RBI sought to meet was clearly laid out. "To be Reformed is to be interested in education—in education from the kindergarten to the university. For some reason one point in the educational program has been given scant consideration by Reformed America. We refer to Bible institute activity...The Reformed Bible Institute seeks to fill the thus far neglected gap in our educational program."

Mark Fakkema would later note that the founding of the Reformed Bible Institute did not come about lightly and stressed this opinion in his remarks at a public meeting for the new school on January 3, 1940.

We believe that this movement is not the result of cold calculation. We believe that this movement was not laid upon us by relentless necessity. God has laid it upon the hearts of many to make the cause of the RBI a subject of prayer. One student mentioned, after leaving classes one evening, "This is something that I have been praying for for twenty years." Speaking of the origin of the RBI movement, we have repeatedly heard the remark, "It was an answer to prayer." Believing that God has laid this matter on the hearts of His people, we are hopeful for the future. For God has a way of answering the prayers which He Himself has laid upon the hearts of His people that it may be abundantly evident that of Him, through Him, and unto Him are all things.

## The 1939 Purpose of the Reformed Bible Institute

The article in the July/August 1939 issue of *The Young Calvinist* included this description of purpose of the Reformed Bible Institute:

The purpose of the Reformed Bible Institute is to provide such systematic Christian training as is not provided elsewhere in our Reformed circles, namely:

1. Systematic training for those who for their own personal development desire to increase their personal knowledge of the Bible and of our Reformed principles, which training is to complement what the church offers;

2. Systematic training for those who would equip themselves spiritually as well as intellectually for the Christian pursuit of whatever their calling in life may be;

3. Systematic training for lay leadership in the church in its various local activities;

4. Systematic training for those who wish to equip themselves for teaching the Bible in the home, in Sunday School, etc.;

5. Systematic training for unordained missionaries and other lay workers who wish to prepare for various phases of evangelistic work.

In making this unique five-point contribution to our educational program consideration shall be given to theory as well as practice, content as well as method.

Spiritual as well as material benefits were also laid out in detail. "The RBI promises its students especially four benefits:

a. It will help to equip them with a better knowledge of the Bible.

b. It will stimulate their interest in the work of the Kingdom of God.

c. It will afford opportunity for a type of fellowship which is rooted in a common interest in the Word of God and in the work of God.

d. It will offer courses and activities that will definitely tend to the deepening of a student's own spiritual life.

[As for material benefits,] The Institute does not promise its students a field of labor upon graduation, although there is a demand for trained workers. It promises to its graduates nothing but the assurance that if they will commit their ways to the Lord, He will direct their paths. It seeks to serve that person who needs the training it offers in order to realize the purpose of God with his life.

## The School is Formed and Studies Begin

Once it was settled that the Reformed Bible Institute would make its home in Grand Rapids, Michigan, the board worked quickly to find a suitable space. They decided

The first location of the Reformed Bible Institute was at 706-708 Wealthy Street on the second floor of a building above En's Cafe.

to rent a place temporarily due to the quickly approaching start date of the school, first slated for September 1939, and search for a more permanent location as time permitted. The start date would eventually be pushed back to January 1940, and beginning that month, RBI rented the second floor at 706–708 Wealthy Street SE in Grand Rapids, above the En's Cafe, for $25 a month.

The Wealthy Street building was owned by a Christian businessman who showed a real interest in the school, and the building was carefully prepared for its new purpose. One room was to be used as a classroom and chapel, one room was to be used as a classroom and library, and an eight-room dormitory across the hall was prepared for female students that included a kitchen, dining room, reception room, and bedrooms for the women. New flooring was put in, the quarters were repainted and redecorated, and light fixtures were installed.

The dining room in the dormitory above En's Cafe in January 1940 was filled with furniture donated to the school by supporters.

The living space in the dormitory was homey and comfortable as pictured in January 1940.

## Rally to Precede Opening of Bible Institute Course

In preparation for the opening of the new Reformed Bible institute, a public rally will be held at 8 o'clock Wednesday evening at the Sherman Street Christian Reformed church. Officers and board members of the institution will explain its purposes.

On the program are President H. J. Kuiper, Secretary Mark Fakkema of Chicago, Johanna Timmer, dean of the school; Rev. Oren Holtrop of Rochester, N. Y., and Rev. J. VanderPloeg of Pella, Iowa. Rev. J. C. DeKorne, vice president, will preside, Agnes Vellenga, member of the board, will offer vocal selections, and Rev. C. M. Schooland of Holland will lead a hymn sing.

The institute, which seeks to fill a need in the Christian Reformed denomination, will provide systematic training for those who seek increased knowledge of the Bible and Reformed principles; for lay leadership in the church, for those who wish to become Bible teachers and for unordained missionaries and other lay workers.

Registration will start Thursday at the institute, which is located at 706-708 Wealthy-st., S. E. There will be no charge for tuition but a nominal registration fee and small yearly membership dues are required. The course is open to high school graduates and persons more than 18 years old.

This undated newspaper article announces the January 3 rally kicking off the start of the first school year.

On January 3, 1940, an open public meeting was held at Sherman Street Christian Reformed Church in Grand Rapids (board member Rev. William Van Peursem was the pastor). Board member Mark Fakkema spoke, outlining the felt need to train Christian lay workers and for systematic Bible study. After outlining the historical roots of the school, he noted, "There was something more to the movement than a mere desire for training and a mere desire to obtain knowledge. The utility motive and the intellectual motive were steeped in religious fervor and Christian consecration."

The next day, registration was held for both day and evening classes and day classes began. As Johanna Timmer reported in the March 1941 *RBI Quarterly*, "The Reformed Bible Institute began its class work on January 4, 1940, with an enrollment of 21 students in the day school and 51 students enrolled in the evening school." As planned, no tuition was charged, but there was a nominal $10 registration fee that covered the entire three-year program.

## Johanna Timmer

One of the founding board members present at the March 28, 1939, meeting of visionaries was the dean of women at Calvin College, Johanna Timmer. Timmer had, earlier in her life, felt the calling to mission work, but health issues prevented her from going overseas. Instead, she pursued a career in teaching and became the first woman faculty member of Calvin College where she taught English and German. She had an AB (bachelor of arts) from Calvin and an AM (master of arts) from the University of Michigan.

Despite health issues, Timmer maintained an interest in missions

The first class of day school students posed for a picture in front of the first RBI building on Wealthy Street on January 4, 1940, the first day of classes.

Johanna Timmer is pictured here in 1946. Timmer was a founding board member and the first full-time instructor at the school.

Nella Mierop was hired in 1942 as the school's second full-time faculty member as a music teacher.

throughout her lifetime, and it was no surprise her interest drew her to Kuiper's home on March 28, 1939, when the Reformed Bible Institute was founded. At the request of that group at that meeting, she became the spokesperson for the newly formed institute and traveled around the country in the second half of 1939, speaking to Reformed church groups to garner support and recruit the first class of students. By December 1939, she had signed up a class of potential students.

The board commended Timmer in the April 27, 1939, edition of *The Banner*: "We bespeak a hearty welcome to Miss Timmer as she begins this adventurous bit of kingdom work. She is to do pioneer work in the launching of a new venture in the educational field. If this movement is successful it will give a great impetus to various types of Christian work within our own circles. And it should prove to be a great blessing in our missionary activities."

December of 1939 was when Timmer's role began to change. From a recruiter and apologist for the idea of a Bible institute, she became a teacher and the acting head of the school. Timmer taught a variety of subjects and enlisted the part-time help of area pastors to augment the curriculum. She also served as dean of students, counselor, and administrator for the school during its critical early years.

Timmer was a much loved and admired teacher. Katie Gunnink (1944), one of Timmer's first RBI students and later a faculty member, remembered this about her: "Those of us who knew her as teacher were impressed with her love for God's Word and the Reformed faith. She taught with such conviction and enthusiasm that the doctrines of the Bible became alive and precious. She taught with great thoroughness, and asked of us such mastery of the truths she presented as to make them permanent possessions of our minds and hearts."

During her time as dean of women at Calvin College and later at the Reformed Bible Institute, Timmer met with some criticism over the strict rules and regulations she enforced such as instructions on attire, curfews, dating policies, and household responsibilities. However, Dick Harms in an article of the *Spark* publication of Calvin College in the summer of 2005 points out she had patterned them after the regulations of other colleges including Hope College and the University of Michigan. Regulations for college life were quite different than those for students today—especially for female students.

A close friend of Timmer, Nella Mierop, became the second full-time faculty member

Nella Mierop (right) was a good friend of Johanna Timmer (left). After the two left RBI they lived and worked together in California and Pennsylvania before coming back to west Michigan.

in 1942 and taught music classes along with instrument lessons. Timmer and Mierop would from then on live and work together, from Grand Rapids, to California, to Pennsylvania, and back to west Michigan.

Timmer remained acting head of the school until the appointment of Rev. Dick H. Walters in 1943. After Walters's appointment, she continued to teach, lead deputation teams of students to supporting churches, and counsel the students until 1951, when she and Mierop left together to teach in Ripon, California. In 1957, Timmer accepted a position as the teaching principal at the Philadelphia-Montgomery Christian High School in Pennsylvania. She died in Holland, Michigan, in January 1978 at the age of seventy-six. The academic building at the 1869 Robinson Road campus was named after her in 1977, and today, the residence building Timmer Hall on the current campus is named after her in recognition of her work during the early days of the Reformed Bible Institute.

"Confident that our church needs the kind of service the Reformed Bible Institute is rendering, confident that the Lord is blessing our feeble efforts, and confident that many of God's people will continue to support it materially, and prayerfully, we face the future with joy, knowing that the Lord will lead in a manner that will glorify him," stated Timmer boldly in the March 1941 *RBI Quarterly*.

## "We His Servants Will Arise and Build"

When the first RBI stationery was printed, the message of Nehemiah 2:20 (KJV) was placed on it: "The God of heaven, he will prosper us; therefore, we his servants will arise and build." This verse became the school's early motto, and all connected to the

# The Reformed Bible Institute

706-8—714-16 WEALTHY ST., S.E.
GRAND RAPIDS, MICHIGAN

*The God of heaven, he will
prosper us; therefore we
his servants will arise and
build . . .*—NEHEMIAH 2:20

Address replies to
1512 So. 57th Ave.,
Cicero, Illinois

April 12, 1941

Dear Fellow-worker:

The R.B.I. Board is planning an annual meeting of all its members to be held in Grand Rapids in the first week of June.

This being the first annual meeting of this new Kingdom cause, important matters pertaining to the policy and future of our Institute will come up for discussion and decision. A permanent board will also be appointed at that time.

The present tentative board has taken the liberty of suggesting your name as a candidate for board membership. From a number of candidates the board of the R.B.I. is to be chosen.

We now come to you with the request that we be permitted to put your name upon the list of candidates. We realize that it is difficult for you to decide in advance whether or not you would be able to serve as a board member since the activities of the board must still be determined at the coming annual meeting. For the sake of saving expense, board meetings will be reduced to a minimum and those living a distance from the center will be asked to function through correspondence.

If we do not hear from you to the contrary within the next couple weeks, we will consider you as one of our candidates for board membership. If under no circumstances, however favorable, you could serve as a board member, we would like to hear from you within the next ten days. We of course would like to have you attend the coming annual meeting and help us work out the future policies of our Institute. We however do not like to have it be understood that attendance is a condition of board membership.

Commending this cause to your prayerful consideration as well as Christian generosity, we are,

Yours in name of the present tentative Board,

*Mark Fakkema*

MF:CV

PS. Any communications touching the above matters may be directed to the present secretary, Mr. Mark Fakkema, 10119 Lafayette Ave., Chicago, Ill.

The first stationery printed for the RBI included the verse from Nehemiah 2:20. This 1941 letter from Board Member Mark Fakkema was sent to a potential board member.

The first teachers of the RBI are pictured here on January 4, 1940: (left to right) Dr. William Hendricksen, Johanna Timmer, and Rev. William Van Peursem. Rev. Cornelius Schoolland, an evening school teacher, is not pictured.

Students pose for a picture after the completion of their first exams on March 21, 1940. From left to right: Johanna Timmer, Bertha Vander Pol, Wilhelmina Tuit, Jessie Sytsma, Mabel Stegink, Gertrude Kuipers, Hattie Veurink, Ethel Lammers, Evelyn Hendee, Elmer De Jong, Marguerite Bonnema, Mary De Boer, Sarah Fredricks, and Alice Elzinga.

Some of the very first day school students study in June 1940.

RBI leaned on the truth it offered. The fledgling school was off and running— but not without the blessing of the Lord.

In addition to Johanna Timmer, who taught most of the classes during the first few years, three other area pastors agreed to teach classes at the new school. Rev. William Van Peursem, a board member and the pastor of Sherman Street Christian Reformed Church in Grand Rapids, taught "The Gospels" at the day school, and Rev. William Hendricksen, who would later teach at Calvin Theological Seminary and publish several commentaries on the New Testament, taught "Bible Introduction." Rev. Cornelius Schoolland, pastor of Harderwyk Christian Reformed Church in Holland, Michigan, taught "Personal Evangelism" in the evenings.

The complete course list for the first term of the day school, beginning in January 1940 consisted of:

- Bible Introduction—2 hours
- The Gospels—1 hour
- Principles of Missions—2 hours
- Bible Doctrine—2 hours
- English—4 hours
- Bible History—1 hour
- Observation—3 hours

Evening school class list:

- Personal Evangelism—1 hour
- Bible Doctrine—1 hour
- English—1 hour

More room for classroom space was soon needed due to the speed with which the board rented the first classroom and dormitory space at 706-708 Wealthy Street. So, in October of 1940, the school rented the second floor of a nearby building at 714 Wealthy Street, two doors east of the main building. This space was used as an additional dormitory space for women

Students met regularly for chapel studies.

Evening school students pose for a picture in June 1940.

The first and second classes of RBI students along with faculty and staff members pose for a picture in October 1940.

and was used until the school purchased 330 Eastern Avenue in September 1942.

The building at 330 Eastern Avenue was purchased from the YMCA for a sum of $6,000, for which the RBI took out a loan for $5,500. The loan was soon paid off, and the building was used as a dormitory for about thirty women and as office space for the institution. When the Eastern Avenue building was purchased, the school stopped renting the 714 Wealthy Street dormitory and began using the space at 706–708 Wealthy Street as classrooms only.

The school received an additional boost and sense of credibility in July 1942 when the Synod of the Christian Reformed Church approved RBI as a recommended cause for giving. This action followed three postponements by the CRC on the issue, but the RBI now had an additional recognition within the denomination along with another source for donations.

## Student Life

The first classes of Reformed Bible Institute students were made up of mostly women and a few men from across the United States and Canada. Of the students in the inaugural class, eleven young women made arrangements to use the dormitories provided by the school in the 706–708 Wealthy Street building. The women lived cheerfully together in the comfortable space furnished with donations of both furniture and money.

The women who elected to live on-campus spent much of their days together. "For nourishment around the table then we meet, and feel anew the joy of Christian love that binds us here together...when breakfast is over, dishes washed, beds all made and rooms in order, we wend our way to class," shared student Margaret Pakkebier, a day school student from Luctor, Kansas, in the March 1949 issue of the *RBI Quarterly*.

"We regard our life at the dormitory as an important element in our training to become more efficient workers in the Kingdom of God," noted senior Wilhelmina Tuit in the same publication. "We strive to make our home what it ought to be. Though in weaknesses and frailties, mistakes and failures, yet with faith and courage, and in the strength of our heavenly Father, we press onward."

Students study on the roof of the classroom building at 706 Wealthy Street.

Students would normally eat meals together in the dormitory's formal dining room.

DORMITORY RULES

"Christ is the Head of this house,
The Unseen Guest at every meal,
The Silent Listener to every conversation."

Live in a consciousness of His ever-abiding presence.

II. Dormitory Schedule:

| | | | |
|---|---|---|---|
| 6:00 A.M. [6:15] | Rising bell | (7:00 A.M. on Saturday and Sunday) | |
| 6:30-7:00 A.M. | Private devotions | (7:30 A.M.    "    "    "    " ) | |
| 7:00-7:20 A.M. | Breakfast | (8:00 A.M.    "    "    "    " ) | |
| 7:20 A.M. | Cleaning | | |
| 12:30 P.M. | Lunch | (12:45 P.M. Sunday dinner) | |
| 2:00-4:30 P.M. | Study period | | |
| 6:00 P.M. | Dinner | ( 5:15 P.M. Sunday supper) | |
| 7:00-9:30 P.M. | Study period (No evening study hours on Friday and Saturday except during examination period.) | | |
| 10:00-10:30 P.M. | Private devotions | | |
| 11:00 P.M. | Lights out (12:00 on Friday evening) | | |

It is not permissible to get up before the rising bell rings, not even during examination time. With permission, one may rise a little earlier on Saturday morning if necessary for her work.

After the morning devotions, come down to the dining room promptly for break-fast. Lunch and dinner will be announced by a bell five minutes before the meal is served and a second bell when ready to serve. Plan to be in the living room at the dormitory when the first bell rings, where you should wait until the final bell rings.

Female students were kept on a tight schedule in the early years of the institute...but sometimes those strict rules were questioned by students.

Johanna Timmer, the head of the institute, supervised dormitory life with a firm but kind hand. She emphasized that activities should be conducted in an orderly fashion, and on-campus students adhered to a strict schedule. The morning bell would ring at 6:00 a.m., and students would arise and participate in a time of personal devotions from 6:30 to 7:00, when breakfast was served. After breakfast, students tidied up and readied themselves for the school day, which would begin at 8:00. Meals were served at noon and 6:00 p.m., and lights out was at 11:00, following another half-hour set aside for personal devotions. On weekends, the morning bell would ring one hour later than usual.

Each morning as part of their schoolwork, students and teachers would come together for an hour-long chapel. Students sometimes would lead the group as part of their training, but often ministers, missionaries, or members of area churches would come and speak. Through these interactions, students were exposed to a variety of activities of the Christian Reformed Church at home and around the world.

## The First Graduating Class

Students Marguerite Bonnema (left) and Dinah Van Dyken (right) pose for a picture in June 1941.

In December 1942, the first class of eleven students—ten women and one man—completed the three-year program. The first graduates were Marguerite Bonnema, Mary Cook, Mary De Boer, Elmer De Jong, Alice Elzinga, Sarah Fredricks, Ethel Lammers, Jessie Sytsma, Wilhelmina Tuit, Bertha Van de Pol, and Hattie Veurink. Classes included Bible Doctrine, Bible History, Bible Introduction, Minor Prophets, Gospel of John, Revelation, Child Study, Christian Ethics, English, The Gospels, Interpretive Reading, Fundamentalism, Modernism, Christian Reformed Missions, Domestic Missions, Foreign Missions, Music, Personal Evangelism, Practical Assignments, Principles of Missions, Public Speaking, Religions of

The first class of eleven students graduated from the Reformed Bible Institute in December 1942.

# The Beginnings of
# Bethany Christian Services

*Reflections from Mary DeBoer VandenBosch, a graduate of the first class in 1942 and one of the founders of Bethany Christian Services. These memories were written in 1998.*

Before I came to RBI, it was my desire to someday have a Christian home for needy children. There were many questions—such as, how does one get started? Where would I find someone else who might have a similar interest? When I heard about RBI's plan to open in January 1940, I was interested. I prayed about it, and I enrolled as a member of that first class.

I was assigned to share a very small room with Marguerite Bonnema, an R.N. from Cleveland, Ohio. The room had a small table, a desk, two chairs, and a bunk bed.

After we had been together for a couple of weeks, Marguerite asked me one day, "What do you plan to do when you finish here?" I replied that I would like to start a Christian home for needy children. But I don't know if I will be able to do that.

Marguerite answered, "That's what I want to do too!" See how wonderfully God's hand is seen in this happening— and what a role RBI played.

After our graduation from RBI, we both worked in city missions for about two years. Marguerite worked in the Broadway Mission and I in West Fulton. During this time, we met Andrew VanderVeer. He, too, became interested, and as you probably already guessed, Bethany Christian Home (now Bethany Christian Services) was begun.

*Today, Bethany is a global nonprofit organization caring for orphans and vulnerable children on five continents through adoptions, foster care, sponsorships, pregnancy counseling, and more. Bethany is recognized as a prominent leader in social services worldwide and is the largest adoption agency in the United States.*

Marguerite Bonnema (left) and Mary DeBoer (right) pose in front of the Wealthy Street classroom with classmate Elmer DeJong. Bonnema and DeBoer, with the assistance of Andrew VanderVeer, would go on to found the organization that is now known as Bethany Christian Services.

of History, Church History, Anti-Christian Faiths, Storytelling, First Aid, and Nursing. Convocation was held on December 17, 1942, and Johanna Timmer gave the address:

It takes spiritual courage to go out into the world as a reformed worker. Your views will be rejected many a time as antiquated relics of a dark religious age...Wherever the Lord leads you and whatever he bids you do, there will be abundant opportunity for sacrificial service.

The way of truth is the way of complete self-giving and self-denial. It is the way of cross-bearing and faith-witnessing. It is the way of clinging tenaciously to sound doctrine and consistently Christian living. May the Lord bless you, keep you, cause His face to shine upon you and give you peace—the peace Jesus came to bring as the Prince of Peace.

The first commencement ceremony of the Reformed Bible Institute was held in the sanctuary of the Sherman Street Christian Reformed Church on December 17, 1942.

THE FIRST

COMMENCEMENT EXERCISES

*of*

*The Reformed Bible Institute*

*and*

THE THIRD

*Founders Day Celebration*

December 17, 1942, 8:00 P. M.

SHERMAN STREET CHRISTIAN REFORMED CHURCH

Grand Rapids, Michigan

The school purchased this home at 330 Eastern Avenue in September 1942 for $6,000. The building was used as a dormitory for women and office space for school administrators until it was sold in 1947.

## Chapter 3

# "The God of Heaven, He Will Prosper Us:" 1943–1957

After the first class of the new school graduated, the RBI base of students, faculty, and supporters continued to grow. Graduates were beginning to serve in various locations throughout the city of Grand Rapids and across the United States as mission workers, teachers, and nurses. In 1942, the Christian Reformed Church Synod made a decision to recommend the RBI to the churches for moral and financial support. People who before did not see the need for a school for lay workers in the church could now begin to see the clear purpose and vision for the institute.

In addition to financial support from the CRC denomination, RBI also instituted a "Pay-a-Day Patron Plan" to raise funds. Interested individuals and organizations could donate $40 to pay for the school's expenses for one day, payable in one lump sum or in four payments of $10 each. Students continued to attend RBI tuition free and could elect to pay about $7.00 a week to stay in campus housing.

During the early years of its existence, the institute had to deal with the effects of World War II. The student body until the mid-1950s was overwhelmingly female for two reasons. First, some men who wanted to go into ministry went to seminary, and secondly, many men were drafted into the army. Elmer De Jong, the only male student from the first class of graduates in 1942, was drafted into military service, as well as other male students that came after him.

Despite World War II, the school continued to flourish. In an article in the December 1943 *RBI Quarterly*, Rev. Emo Van Halsema (whose son, Dr. Dick L. Van Halsema, would later become president of RBI) wrote about the movement for Reformed Bible institutes and its effectiveness in Grand Rapids and at other similar institutions. "In training and equipping for witness-bearing, the RBI serves a blessed purpose in the church. Then, the RBI serves the more immediate purpose of training workers for the Sunday School, for the Mission field, and for other positions of trust and leadership in the church of Christ," he wrote. "May the RBI be instrumental in sending forth an abundance of white corpuscles into the bloodstream of the church for buoyant, vigorous spiritual health and to the glory of God."

During WWII, several students were drafted into military service, including the school's first male graduate, Elmer DeJong (1942), far left.

# Other Reformed Bible Institutes in the United States

As the Reformed Bible Institute in Grand Rapids gained its footing, other similar institutions were forming across the United States. Interest in missions and evangelism was rapidly increasing through the 1940s and many small schools offered classes to train students of all ages to spread the good news of the gospel.

The Eastern Reformed Bible Institute flourished in New Jersey in the early 1940s. The school only held evening classes, yet its purpose was very similar to the Grand Rapids RBI: to train laypeople in the Reformed tradition. Local pastors and teachers taught classes and courses included Reformed Doctrine, The Life of Christ, and Church History. Though the schools were not affiliated in any way, there was amiable communication between the Grand Rapids school and the New Jersey school.

A Reformed Bible Institute Evening School was also active in Chicago, and Grand Rapids RBI board member Mark Fakkema, who lived in Chicago, taught several classes. Course titles included Christian Testimony, Epistles of John, and The Gospel in the Old Testament. In 1943, fifty-four students were enrolled in the Chicago RBI.

A Reformed Bible Institute of Southern California also existed in the 1940s. Evening classes were held for lay leaders in the church and for those who desired to increase their knowledge of the Bible and of Reformed principles.

Along with the schools that existed in New Jersey, Chicago, and California, independent classes were held in Kalamazoo and in other areas in west Michigan by various church and mission organizations. Interest in evangelistic work was quickly gaining momentum.

The class of 1943 is pictured with teachers Johanna Timmer and Rolf Veenstra.

## Rev. Dick H. Walters Appointed First President

Once classes began in 1940, discussion continued among the board as to when a president should be appointed to lead the fledgling school. During 1942, several competent leaders were considered, and some were even offered the position but declined. In June 1943, the board voted to call Rev. Dick H. Walters, who was then the pastor of Central Avenue Christian Reformed Church in Holland, Michigan. Walters was offered a salary of $2,500 a year and free housing.

Rev. Walters accepted the appointment and became the Reformed Bible Institute's first president. Before he began, someone once asked him if he should be leaving a church of 1,300 to serve at an institute of only thirty people. Later, President Walters recalled, "I didn't want to tell them that there was actually only 22 women and 1 man!"

In addition to his administrative duties, President Walters taught several classes and frequently hosted educational programs on local Grand Rapids radio stations. One of the most memorable classes he taught

Rev. Dick H. Walters, formerly the pastor of Central Avenue Christian Reformed Church in Holland, was appointed the first president of the Reformed Bible Institute in June 1943.

Friday

To the R.B.I Board
The Rev. H.J. Kuiper
Bradley, Mich

My dear Kuiper:

I hereby answer your call to the R.B.I. I accept the appointment. I cannot do otherwise; so help me God!

I fully realize that it requires much faith to face that challenge in that appointment, yet within me I'm thrilled at that challenge of faith. I am willing to take the "risk of faith" as one of my people put it.

I have great confidence in the board and the faculty, and I believe the R.B.I. movement was a deeply spiritual one from its very inception. I believe also that it has the spiritual backing of our common people, as soon as they understand what the R.B.I. means.

I promise to put my whole soul into this great work, and I crave your prayers and cooperation.

As president of the board you have presented the matter to me fairly, with no pressure. I am doing only what I believe is the Lord's will for my life.

Anticipating further relations with you,

I am,

Fraternally yours,

Dear Miss Timmer:
Am sending you a copy of my letter to the Board.
Appreciating your help in this period of consideration. You have been fair and spiritual
Walters

Rev. Walters became the first president of the RBI and accepted the position in this letter addressed to the board and Chairman of the Board Rev. H. J. Kuiper. In a handwritten note, he thanks Johanna Timmer for "being fair and spiritual" "during this period of consideration."

until his death was called "The Lordship of Christ." President Walters, along with Rev. John Schaal, would also teach frequently in area churches and travel extensively publicizing the institute. The connections forged on these teaching trips allowed them to work with people who were interested in Bible study and the Sunday School movement in the CRC and enabled them to give students practical ministry assignments.

Rev. Walters served as president until health problems necessitated his retirement in May of 1966. He continued to teach part-time at the school until his sudden death while on his way to chapel on December 11, 1967, his sixtieth birthday.

His successor, Dr. Dick L. Van Halsema recalled, "[Walters] life and labors on behalf of RBI continue to be remembered gratefully by many of his friends and former students. His readiness to quote Romans 11:36 in connection with RBI's ministry and history leads me to conclude with those same words: 'For of Him and through Him and to Him, are all things; to Whom be the glory forever. Amen.'"

## Finding a More Permanent Home

When Walters became president in 1943, the school faced a variety of growth needs. The 330 Eastern Avenue building had been purchased the year before for dormitory space and the school stopped using the 714 Wealthy Street building, continuing to use the space at 706–708 Wealthy Street. In the March 1944 issue of the *RBI Quarterly*, Walters laid out the need for a larger building and proposed a $75,000 building project, and the school began raising money.

Donations poured in quickly, but the board was not willing to take on a large amount of debt, so other solutions were sought. In 1945, the school stopped using its original space at 706–708 Wealthy Street when the board purchased a large house at 1230 Lake Drive, which was used as a classroom building with a library and office and dormitory space in the basement. But only two years later, the school had already outgrown it, and furthermore, the city fire commission ordered expensive alterations be made to the building if it was continued to be used as classroom space. The school then converted the home fully into a women's dormitory for thirty students.

As the need for more space grew more and more urgent into the late 1940s, the board desired to purchase existing space to circumvent the need to build. A large estate at 1869 Robinson Road in Grand Rapids came to the attention of board members Rev. H. J. Kuiper and Rev. William Van Peursem in 1947. The large home and 3½ acres of spacious, manicured grounds were

Because the institute did not yet have a permanent home, President Dick H. Walters began raising money for a $75,000 school building in 1943. Donations were received, but the board was unwilling to take on such a large amount of debt, so other solutions were sought.

The home at 1230 Lake Drive was purchased in 1945 and allowed the school to stop renting the space at 706-708 Wealthy Street.

The house at 1869 Robinson Road was purchased by the RBI in 1947 and included 3½ acres of well-manicured grounds.

This is a view of the rear of the building at 1869 Robinson Road and shows the well-landscaped property. Several additions were added to this building in later years.

owned by Heber W. Curtis, president of the Old Kent Bank at the time (now Fifth Third Bank). Before Curtis, the home was owned by William Alden Smith, a United States Senator from Michigan, who was involved in the investigation into the *Titanic*'s sinking.

The asking price for the landscaped property, which included a scenic pond in front of the residence, was a staggering $120,000. But through the efforts of Kuiper, Van Peursem, and board member Dr. George Broodman, Curtis graciously agreed to lower the purchase price to $60,000. Due to the large amount of donations that had been received since the 1944 building project was proposed, the school only took on a relatively small amount of debt that was paid off quickly. Curtis also helped them finance the debt the institute owed to him, making it easier for the school to move forward.

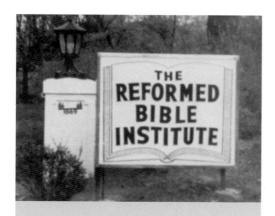

This sign, pictured in 1954, stood at the entrance to the Robinson Road campus the college purchased in 1947.

From 1948 until the move to the East Beltline campus in 1990, the house at 1869 Robinson Road was used for classroom and administration space. The building was named Timmer Hall in the 1970s in honor of Johanna Timmer, the school's first teacher and administrator. Timmer Hall was about a half mile east of the 1230 Lake Drive dormitory, within walking distance.

That same week the home at 1869 Robinson Road and the land surrounding it was purchased, RBI's offer to purchase the home at 1245 Lake Drive (across the street from 1230 Lake Drive) was accepted. Since the 330 Eastern Avenue dormitory was too far from the new campus, the board sold it in 1947.

In the summer 1947 issue of the *RBI Quarterly*, President Walters wrote, "All who remember our humble beginnings in the Wealthy Street 'upper rooms' now marvel at the acquisition of properties which several realtors have termed 'the finest in the city.'" The RBI had grown from its early beginning by enhancing its location and gaining broad visibility in the Grand Rapids area. Now with adequate space, the school could finally settle in and expand on its new campus.

## Correspondence Courses

During the early decades of the Reformed Bible Institute, there were three distinct branches of education occurring at RBI: the day school on campus, popular evening classes in Grand Rapids and in surrounding communities, and correspondence courses for home study—a program which President Walters supported and developed. These correspondence courses were circulated throughout the United States and Canada. Students who enrolled worked on lessons at home and then mailed them to RBI instructors for correction and credit. These correspondence courses were also an effective recruitment tool for the day school.

As the program grew, RBI faculty members continued to write new notes for class lectures, which were used for the correspondence courses. The major work of typing up these notes was done by the faculty secretary and RBI alumna Sarah

Purchased in 1947, the home at 1245 Lake Drive was used as a dormitory until it was sold in the late 1960s. This home was across the street from the school's other dormitory at 1230 Lake Drive.

Fredricks, who was one of the graduates of the first class in 1942. Fredricks would serve until 1972 as secretary for the faculty and two presidents.

The correspondence course program continued until 2005 and was discontinued when online courses became popular. During the later years of the program, a prison ministry developed and often as many as half

Correspondence courses were a large part of the institute's academic offerings and served the needs of students who could not physically attend classes at the school. Wilma Brouwer, one secretary of the correspondence program, is pictured here in the 1960s. The correspondence course program continued into the 2000s.

Sarah Fredricks was a member of the first graduating class of students in 1942 and became the institute's secretary for the faculty and two presidents. She is pictured here just before her retirement in 1972.

of those enrolled in correspondence courses were incarcerated.

## Alumni Work at Home and Around the World

After the first class graduated in December 1942, it took only three months for all to find employment, most of them in the mission field. Jessie Sytsma and Mary De Boer worked in the West Fulton Street Mission, and Wilhelmina Tuit ministered at the Jewish Mission in Chicago. By 1943, graduates were working at the Rehoboth Christian School in Rehoboth, New Mexico, and among Native Americans in Toadlena, New Mexico. Yet another worked at the Cutlerville Psychopathic Hospital (now Pine Rest Christian Mental Health Services) in Grand Rapids.

Many RBI graduates also went on to serve at various "chapels" across the country. These chapels were usually new attempts to share the gospel that might be called "church plants" today and were typically small in size—though many expanded into organized churches and still exist today. RBI alumni worked in chapels across Michigan and in Indiana, Illinois, Wisconsin, Iowa, South Dakota, New Jersey, and as far away as Denver, Colorado. These graduates played a significant role in the outreach and growth of the Christian Reformed Church.

Alumni work also expanded abroad into foreign missions. Alice Elzinga (1942) became the first foreign missionary from RBI when she began work in Suriname in 1944. Jeanette Boersma (1944) became RBI's first foreign missionary nurse in 1945 and worked in a mission hospital in Amarah, Iraq, and in 1946, Margaret Dykstra (1944) began work in Nigeria. Other graduates from the 1940s served as missionaries in China, India, and Bahrain.

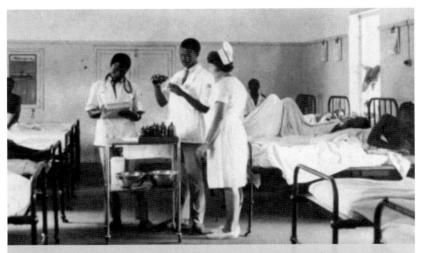

RBI alumna Cloe Ann Danford (1964) worked in Mkar, Nigeria, as a missionary nurse.

graduated from the RBI, went back and completed high school since high school graduation was not a requirement to enroll in RBI in its early years. Other students went on to further education at a variety of educational institutions, including graduate school and seminary.

## Faculty Development

The Reformed Bible Institute was blessed from the beginning with dedicated and passionate faculty members who were not merely teachers but respected leaders in education. Many RBI professors were well-trained professors who taught at other colleges and seminaries either during or after their time at RBI. Others were pastors in area churches who served their churches well and regularly received calls from other churches who sought their services as pastors. Johanna Timmer was the first teacher and administrator of the school, and though she set the bar high, others followed in her footsteps of excellence.

One such teacher was Dr. William Hendriksen, a recognized biblical scholar who wrote a number of commentaries on

Demand for RBI graduates continued to rise in the United States and around the world. The class of 1947 reportedly declined more job offers than they could accept! In 1948, the tally of foreign missionaries from RBI rose to four. Nineteen graduates were working as domestic missionaries and nine were active in Native American ministries. Still others were teachers, nurses, and social service workers.

Many graduates went on to continue their education. Some students, after they

Rev. Dick H. Walters leads a faculty meeting in 1946.

Dr. William Hendricksen was a part-time teacher at the RBI for many years. He became a well-known New Testament scholar and published the book *More Than Conquerors* and several well-known commentaries on the New Testament.

Katie Gunnink was an early graduate of the RBI and served as a member of the faculty from 1944 to 1978. Students recalled her prayers were "masterpieces of the Christian faith."

New Testament books published by Baker Book House. Hendriksen also served on the board and resumed teaching at RBI part-time after he had taught at Calvin Theological Seminary and returned to the pastorate.

Katie Gunnink was another well-respected teacher and a full-time faculty member who served for many years at RBI. Gunnink came to RBI as a student in 1941 to further her education after graduating from Calvin College. While she was a student, she once was asked by Dr. Hendriksen if she would be willing to substitute teach in his Revelation class, which she did well. Upon her graduation in 1944, Johanna Timmer asked her to join the faculty full-time, which she did until her retirement in 1978.

Jack Van Laar served as a music teacher full-time at RBI from 1952 to 1988—thirty-six years. With limited numbers of students to draw from, he still formed and directed numerous choirs. His love for good music was a major influence at RBI and on the lives of his students. In 2005, the Jack Van Laar Endowed Chair of Music and Worship was established in his honor.

Dr. William Masselink began work as the head of the doctrine department in 1952 and served until his retirement in 1964. He was remembered as a "colorful and scholarly member of our faculty" in the Volume 6 No. 3 *RBI Newsletter*.

Jack Van Laar served as a music professor at RBI from 1952 to 1988. He conducted many significant musical events and led choir tours around the country every year.

## Rev. John H. Schaal's Contribution to RBI

In the summer of 1948, Rev. John H. Schaal accepted a position as a full-time instructor at RBI. Schaal was one of the founding board members of the institute and had been serving as the pastor of Second Christian Reformed Church in Fremont, Michigan. Beginning in 1937, Schaal taught at a small mission school in Kalamazoo while he was pastor at the Milwood Christian Reformed Church, so he understood the needs and complexities of the Bible school movement. Schaal was also the editor of the CRC's Sunday School papers and had been on the Christian Reformed Board of Missions.

Schaal would serve in a variety of positions at the school for more than twenty-five years as a faculty member and academic dean. Over the years, Schaal and his wife opened their home to hundreds of students, guiding and counseling. Upon his retirement on December 31, 1973, Schaal's service to the school was noted by a telegram from then-Vice President Gerald R. Ford. Today, a dormitory on campus is named Schaal Hall in his honor.

Rev. John H. Schaal, one of the founding board members of the institute, joined the faculty in 1948 and served in a variety of positions at the school for more than twenty-five years.

RBI has always emphasized the practical application of its education. Students regularly went out into the local community, ministering and sharing the gospel with others.

## Academic Developments and Student Life

During the early years of the institute, educational opportunities expanded and changed quickly. In addition to classes on Bible, theology, evangelism, and missions, other practical classes were added like piano lessons, secretarial and bookkeeping courses, first aid, accounting, and typing.

One unique class was the Practical Assignments Class that began early in the institute's history. Students in the class did fieldwork such as visiting hospitals, teaching children's Bible classes, and neighborhood

Students often ate meals together, as pictured here in 1946. Meals at the school were a formal occasion and table linens and formal dishware were commonly used.

Students regularly participated in and led chapel devotions and worship. "As students we do not always feel qualified to be chapel chairman and to direct the music; but, it is part of our training, and we who have taken part know that the first blessing has been ours," noted one student in the 1946 *Echo* yearbook.

evangelism. These assignments were excellent training for students' later occupations, and a practical element of an education at Kuyper College is still emphasized today.

Another unique aspect of the early years of the RBI was deputation teams. Groups of students would travel throughout west Michigan and the United States to acquaint people with the school and raise support and awareness to the needs of missions and missionaries.

Though coursework took up much of students' time, other extracurricular activities were popular. Many students enjoyed the

fellowship and camaraderie they experienced with students, staff, and faculty. Students could participate in the student council, girls' chorus or choir, and various clubs and social gatherings. The *Echo* yearbook began being published in 1944 by a group of students and was the name of that publication for many decades. Students who lived in the dormitories would regularly meet for devotions and prayer, and the entire school would frequently go on outings like picnics, hayrides, sleigh rides, and trips to Lake Michigan. A Christmas banquet tradition began and continues to this day.

## Chapter 4

# Growth and Growing Pains:
## 1958–1969

The late 1950s and the 1960s were years of both remarkable growth and difficult challenges for the Reformed Bible Institute. Two hundred fifty day school students had graduated by 1960, and evening classes had a weekly enrollment of five to six hundred students. Correspondence courses continued to be popular, and the Reformed Bible Institute Association boasted over ten thousand members. The school was no longer a new endeavor—it was an established, respected school.

Success of the institute can be traced to the school's unique function, the faithfulness of its leadership, and the emphasis placed on the importance of the Bible and evangelism—an emphasis that remains exceedingly evident today. The Spring 1959 school newsletter stated, "We believe the function of the Bible Institute is unique because of the combination of Bible study, Evangelism, Music and lay interest and activity. The Bible is central to the whole curriculum, and each teacher and student aims at proficiency in the handling of the one Book...Our aim is to prepare for Christian Leadership, preserve Faith, proclaim the Word, provide vision, promote godliness—all to the glory of His name."

But there were challenges too. In 1969, the school would face an identity crisis and a precipitous drop in enrollment. Finances were in short supply. Current events like the Vietnam War and the social revolution of the 1960s took a great toll on both the nation and the school. How would the Reformed Bible Institute retain its initial purpose and vision while reinventing itself to meet the needs of the day?

## Building Expansion and Dormitory Acquisitions

In 1958, the school once again had to face the issue of inadequate classroom and dormitory space. The board was committed to creating a campus on the 1869 Robinson Road estate of Heber Curtis, but the school needed more space than provided in the original building and the property. The building had three classrooms, but the blessing of larger and larger class sizes was becoming a problem. Many times, during chapel or evening classes, it was necessary to fit ninety people into a 16 by 38-foot room.

President Dick H. Walters stands in front of the RBI sign on Robinson Road.

*Ron wrote these reflections in 2013. After graduation from RBI, Ron served at pastorates in Alberta, Washington, Vermont, Michigan, and Iowa. After he "retired," Ron and his wife Marlene taught English in China and served three congregations as an interim pastor.*

There is a special letter included with my important papers. It is the letter of acceptance from RBI. My start at RBI is now history, but the story goes on.

My favorite memories of RBI are those which broadened my knowledge, relationships, and God's purpose for my life. My understanding of the Scripture grew through Bible doctrine classes and the memorization of God's Word. It was also broadening to have Mr. David Villa open our class with prayer in Spanish, his native language. Miss Katie Gunnink shaped an appreciation for the gifts God has given to women. Mr. Van Laar formed an appreciation for music. Choir tours to Florida, New York and Wisconsin added to my love for the people of God. All of the instructors used their gifts to be a blessing to me. This was not only a time of formal education, but also a time of inter-generational friendships that have lasted for years.

Another type of broadening came through friendships with students from western Michigan and other areas. I still have very fond memories of classmates from the Navajo and Zuni tribes. Canadians added their richness to my life (after graduation we served a mission church in Alberta, Canada). There were also students from India, Africa, and Japan who so enriched me and gave me much more of a world perspective of God's work.

There are many memories, but the best one came in my last year at RBI. It was my first date with Marlene Compagner (Class of 1962) on Thanksgiving Day. After that night I knew she would be my wife. I didn't know at that time about our almost 50 years of marriage, the four children, and the sixteen grandchildren. That story would unfold throughout the years of mission work, further study for ordination, and ministry!

In February 1958, the institute broke ground on a new classroom and chapel building. Rev. William Van Peursem is pictured here speaking at the groundbreaking event.

The board committed itself to a $100,000 building program to add to the existing space, and ground was broken in February 1958 for three additional classrooms and a chapel. The school was debt free in 1957, so the added expense of the new building was feasible. In the end, the cost for the project was $150,000, 25 percent of which was paid off immediately by donations. The remainder of the cost was paid using a fifteen-year promissory note held by RBI's constituency, so it was not necessary for the school to borrow from a bank.

Construction of the classroom and chapel building on the back of the home (later named Timmer Hall) at 1869 Robinson Road occurred in early 1958 at a cost of $150,000.

The home at 1301 Lake Drive was purchased in 1958 and was used as a dormitory until its sale a decade later.

The library is pictured here in 1959, before a dedicated library space was added to the main building in 1962.

The Reformed Bible Institute maintained ties to the Helping Hand Mission in Chicago, which sponsored a Bible institute there in the 1930s and 1940s. The RBI class of 1958 is pictured here in Chicago in front of the mission.

The building project was completed and ready for use in September 1958. Enrollment immediately increased 15 percent, so the school's good stewardship and wise planning were quickly rewarded.

In 1962, a library addition was added to the main building for $17,000 as part of the process to receive full accreditation. The accrediting agency had noted with concern in 1952 that the school did not have a very substantial library, but the gift of 2,500 books from the estate of H. J. Kuiper and the library addition allayed the agency's concerns.

Between 1966 and 1968, the institute purchased four homes near campus to use as student housing. The dorms were named South, North, East, and West Halls. Because of these purchases, the school was able to sell the houses at 1230, 1245, and 1301 Lake Drive and locate itself on a single campus for the first time since the early 1940s.

RBI students from the 1958–1959 school year pose in front of the school's sign on the new classroom and chapel addition.

A chapel addition to the main building at 1869 Robinson Road was completed in 1958. Here, Dr. Lubbertus Oostendorp is leading a chapel service for the college community. The pipe organ shown in the corner of the chapel was a gift to the college as a tribute to music professor Jack Van Laar.

## Accreditation

Until 1964, the Reformed Bible Institute was not fully accredited by any educational agency, and it was becoming increasingly difficult for students to be admitted to degree-granting colleges or universities. However, the caliber of education students received at RBI was such that a few schools were able to make special arrangements for RBI graduates. Barrington College in Providence, Rhode Island, was one such school that would accept RBI graduates and grant them an AB (bachelor of arts) degree after only one year of study.

In the early 1960s, RBI began pursuing full accreditation through the Accrediting Association of Bible Colleges (now the Association for Biblical Higher Education), from which it had received intermediate accreditation in 1951. The board and faculty members spent much time in thought and prayer as to whether this was the right move to make. They decided to go forward with several site inspections, interviews with AABC representatives, and course adjustment to fit AABC guidelines.

To better fit these guidelines, the school library was expanded and a physical

An addition with three classrooms and a chapel was added to the building at 1869 Robinson Road in 1958.

The classroom and chapel addition included space for students called "The Commons" where students could have fellowship and study. Meeting after chapel for coffee and snacks was one popular use for this space, as pictured here in 1959.

In 1962, the main campus building at 1869 Robinson Road underwent another addition when construction on the library was completed.

This home at 155 Woodward Avenue was one of four purchased in the late 1960s. Their purchase allowed the school to sell the houses on Lake Drive and become more centralized on the 1869 Robinson Road campus.

education program was added to the curriculum in 1964. Another part of the process included submitting a 114-page self-study covering topics like the school's physical space, financial stability, and course content.

The self-study was presented to the AABC and the RBI was granted accreditation in the fall of 1964. The school could now stand on its own merits as an accredited institution. The accreditation was also a directional change as now the school began making plans to add a fourth year to the curriculum so it might begin granting bachelor degrees in the future.

More than three acres near the new classroom addition were purchased and cleared in 1966 for sports fields.

New campus boundaries are outlined indicating new acreage to the north and the new purchase on Woodward Lane. In the foreground is Robinson Road.

This home at 63 Woodward Avenue was one of four purchased in the late 1960s. The four new dormitories were named North, South, East, and West Halls.

## Dr. Dick L. Van Halsema Becomes the Second President

Dr. and Mrs. Van Halsema (left) are welcomed by Rev. and Mrs. Walters and Rev. William VanderHaak (board chairman) in November 1966. Dr. Van Halsema became president in the summer of 1966 and Rev. Walters, the first president of RBI, died in 1967.

Rev. Dick Van Halsema, or "Dr. Van," succeeded Rev. Dick H. Walters as president in the summer of 1966. He is pictured here in 1969.

In May 1966, the first president of the Reformed Bible Institute, Dr. Walters, resigned due to health reasons. The board then appointed the school's dean and fellow board member Rev. John H. Schaal as the interim president and set out to find a new candidate who would fit the qualifications. The board identified several qualifications—most importantly that the president would be dedicated to missions and would be young enough to guide the school for the next generation. Other desires were that he would be a leader in the church, a promoter of missions and Christian education, and would have a doctorate.

It did not take long to find just such a candidate in Dr. Dick L. Van Halsema. Van Halsema received his education at Calvin College and Calvin Seminary and received a doctorate from Union Theological Seminary in New York in 1956. He served from 1943 to 1946 with the United States Army in the Pacific in World War II. Later, from 1952 to 1982, he served as a chaplain in the army reserve and retired with the rank of colonel. Van Halsema traced his passion for preaching and mission work to his time serving in the military.

In 1957, he became the Christian Reformed Church Home Missionary-at-Large and became the first denominational minister of evangelism in 1959. From 1963 to 1966, Van Halsema was the pastor of

Central Avenue Christian Reformed Church in Holland, Michigan (Dr. Walters, the first president of the RBI, pastored the same church before his time as president).

"Dr. Van," as he was called, began his work at the Reformed Bible Institute in the summer of 1966. Under his leadership, RBI agreed to function as the publisher of *Missionary Monthly* magazine, of which Van Halsema was the editor (the editor before Van Halsema was Dr. John C. DeKorne, one of the founding board members of RBI). The school served as the publisher of the magazine until Van Halsema's retirement in 1987.

Van Halsema and his wife Thea, who served alongside her husband beginning in the early 1970s as the dean of students and taught in the social work department, also helped to increase the school's enrollment of international students. The couple frequently traveled abroad and made many connections for the college. Financial support for international students came from a growing number of scholarships and from funds solicited from *Missionary Monthly* readers. The new president also connected the Reformed Bible Institute with well-known speakers and organizations such as J. I. Packer, John R. W. Stott, Elizabeth Elliot, Dr. Roger Greenway, and Wycliffe Translators.

## Summer Training Sessions

Van Halsema honed the school's focus toward missions during his tenure by creating the Summer Training Session (STS) program in 1968. STS was a chance for students to serve abroad doing mission work for two months in the summer.

The first STS was held in Mexico and included exposure to another culture, instruction in the Spanish language, and field training assignments in many parts of

Thea Van Halsema, President Van Halsema's wife, joined the faculty in 1972 as a social work instructor. She also served as dean of women.

RBI consciously recruited students from other countries around the world. Pictured here are international students in 1964.

## REFORMED BIBLE COLLEGE

1869 ROBINSON ROAD S.E. GRAND RAPIDS MICHIGAN 49506 458-0404 Cable Address: REFBICO

**RBC**

FIELD TRAINING PROGRAMS

**STS**

MEXICO SUMMER TRAINING SESSION

**TASC**

TRAINING AND SERVICE CORPS

**METS**

MIDDLE EAST TRAINING SESSION

Many students participated in Summer Training Sessions to Mexico led by President Dick Van Halsema. Pictured is a student on the first trip in 1968.

Mexico. Academic credit was given for the two-month program. Though there were tough requirements for acceptance, twenty-two college students went on the first STS—nine from RBI and others from Calvin College, Grand Valley State University, and elsewhere. Fifty-four students went on the second STS to Mexico in 1969. The program continued into the 1990s.

Van Halsema also developed the Middle East Training Session (METS) and the Training and Service Corps (TASC). METS was introduced in 1979 and involved academic courses and fieldwork in the Middle East. TASC began in 1976 and involved a two-year period of mission study and service. TASC participants were generally required to have graduated from

college and have completed the STS program or the METS program.

One huge blessing of these programs was the interest generated for Reformed Bible College (the name of the institute changed in 1971). Over one ten-year period, the STS had more than five hundred students participate. Students were attracted to and attended the college because of these unique programs. Many RBC students who participated in these programs went on to work in mission positions sponsored by the Christian Reformed Church and other organizations—in 1993, it was estimated a staggering 60 percent of current CRC missionaries had attended RBC at some point.

## The Expanding Nature of the Reformed Bible Institute

As the institute grew and flourished, faculty members continued the founders' legacy of reaching out beyond the campus to educate laypeople. Correspondence

RBC became well known for its field training programs including the Summer Training Session (STS), Training and Service Corps (TASC), and Middle East Training Session (METS).

courses continued to be very popular in the United States and Canada. Evening classes conducted by faculty members continued and spread throughout western and northern Michigan in the 1960s with classes in cities like Holland, Zeeland, Grand Haven, Kalamazoo, Fremont, Muskegon, and McBain. Katie Gunnink, William Masselink, John Schaal, and Dick Walters constantly traveled to church groups, Sunday School teachers' meetings, and groups interested in Bible study.

But the reach of the Reformed Bible Institute was not limited to Michigan. In 1967, summer sessions were held in places like Denver, Colorado; Vancouver, British Columbia; and Edmonton, Alberta. In 1968, RBI faculty members taught summer sessions in Paterson, New Jersey, and Whitinsville,

Joanne Boehm served as the college librarian from 1966 to 1985.

This 1965 faculty photo shows (left to right) Katie Gunnink, Jack Van Laar, Rev. Dick H. Walters, Rev. Rolf Veenstra, Wilma Brouwer, Rev. John Schaal, Dr. Lubbertus Oostendorp, and Jack Stoepker.

Students exit the classroom section of the institute during a Michigan winter.

Massachusetts. On Sundays, the faculty members teaching these sessions preached and spoke in area churches.

Faculty members were also active in the Midwest Sunday School Association through John Schaal's encouragement. Schaal served as the editor of the Christian Reformed Church Sunday School papers for twenty-five years and would recruit RBI faculty to be speakers and leaders in that organization.

Several new staff and faculty members began their work at RBI during this era. Joanne Boehm served as the librarian from 1966 to 1985 and processed thousands of books, many donated by the family of H. J. Kuiper. Rev. Lubbertus Oostendorp joined the faculty full-time in 1964 and taught Bible and theology. Rev. Rolf Veenstra also began working full-time at RBI in 1964 as a missions professor. Both Oostendorp and

"There was reason for excitement in the halls of RBI this year. For the first time in history our school was represented by a basketball team...The team did not have great success during its first year, but the students had many exciting moments cheering for the team." Source: 1966 Echo

The 1967 RBI Board of Directors is pictured after President Walters retired but before his death in December 1967. The officers are seated (left to right): C. Westenbroek (treasurer), Rev. William VanderHaak (president), Rev. John H. Schaal (dean and acting president of the institute), Rev. Dick H. Walters (president emeritus), Mrs. Emo Van Halsema (secretary and mother of Dr. Dick Van Halsema), and Alvin Huibregtse (vice president).

Veenstra had taught on a part-time basis in the early years of the institute. In 1969, Harold Bruxvoort joined the faculty as an English and literature professor. He would later serve as the academic dean after Dr. John Schaal retired.

## Growing Pains

Though the 1960s were years of remarkable growth for the Reformed Bible Institute, the end of the decade brought about new difficulties and questions about the future. A dramatic drop in enrollment left only sixty-eight students on campus in 1969—the lowest point since 1954. At the same time, financial support began to wane. A stubborn deficit and lack of funds meant serious questions began to be asked among the faculty and board about the future of the institution. Some even suggested the school should close.

"The last few years prior to 1970 were heart-searching years," Katie Gunnink later wrote. "Would we hold to RBI's original purpose of training lay men and women for

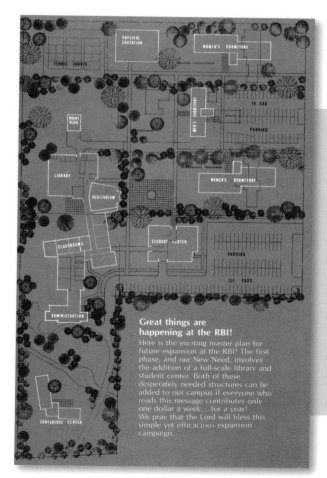

**Great things are happening at the RBI!**

Here is the exciting master plan for future expansion at the RBI! The first phase, and our New Need, involves the addition of a full-scale library and student center. Both of these desperately needed structures can be added to our campus if everyone who reads this message contributes only one dollar a week... for a year! We pray that the Lord will bless this simple yet efficacious expansion campaign.

The institute prepared a master plan for campus expansion in 1969. A number of the concepts on this proposed plan such as a conference center, a library and auditorium, and a second dormitory were never accomplished because of the financial difficulties faced in the late 1960s and early 1970s and opposition from neighbors during the 1980s.

Students are gathered in front of one of the dormitories on Woodward Lane. The homes acquired by the college were some of the nicest historic homes in the Grand Rapids market.

ministries in church and mission, or would we become a Bible conference center or other kind of institution?"

President Van Halsema recalled these difficult years as well. "At one discussion the chairman of the finance committee wept as he described how critical were RBC's needs for students and money.

"So we went to work with a will—faculty, staff, trustees, alumni, and friends of the college all praying and cooperating for its progress. We praised God for His blessing, because within a few years the newly-approved degree-granting college had both more students and increased financial support."

Students often took advantage of the well-manicured landscaping of the 1869 Robinson Road campus as pictured here in 1961.

Students regularly gathered for meals in the main building on the 1869 Robinson Road campus as shown here in 1968.

# Chapter 5

# The Change from Institute to College: 1970–1980

"We hear about miracles now and then, but from July 1 to December 31, a miracle really took place in RBI's finances," reported the January 1970 *R.B.I. Newsletter.* During a deep financial crisis during the late 1960s, the institute faced a myriad of questions about the future of the school. Several urgent pleas for support went out, and the Lord soon answered prayers in a mighty way: from July 1 to December 31, 1969, donations from individuals swelled to a total of $67,685 (compared to $35,550 in the same period the year before) and donations from churches totaled $26,264 (compared to $16,633 a year before).

To address the drop in enrollment and the financial crisis, the board appointed a special committee to study the causes and to suggest solutions. Though only four students graduated from the RBI in May 1970, forty-four new students enrolled the following September and a record 167 students enrolled in September 1972. God had more in store for the RBI, and the 1970s would bring about big changes for the institute.

## Bachelor of Religious Education Degree

During the 1960s, the RBI board and faculty members expressed a vision of improving the school by implementing a four-year course from which a student could earn a bachelor of religious education degree. In the Spring 1967 *R.B.I. Newsletter*, President Van Halsema explained the vision and why it was important. "The B.R.E. program would be specialized, emphasizing courses in Bible as before, with greater course offerings in evangelism, missions, religious education, language, and other areas. In this sense, it would be distinct from a liberal arts college education, by which a student prepares for his life's work in the ministry, education and other fields."

Dean and faculty member John Schaal spearheaded the effort, which involved a seventy-five-page document requesting approval for a four-year degree program. The proposal was submitted to the Michigan State Board of Education in December 1967. However, several tumultuous years would go by before the school would receive an answer. Finally, on June 10, 1970, the State Board of Education approved RBI's four-year degree program.

"Dr. Van," as President Dick L. Van Halsema was called, is pictured here in 1973 in the president's office in Timmer Hall.

## Reformed Bible Institute Becomes Reformed Bible College

RBI alumnus Henry Boehm (1960) served as an evangelist at Windfall Chapel in Grant, Michigan. Many RBI graduates went on to serve as chapel evangelists, and many of those chapels became established churches.

In May 1971, the Reformed Bible Institute Board of Trustees voted to ask the RBI Association members for a unique request: to change the name of the school to Reformed Bible College. The new name would better reflect the school's status as a degree-granting institution since the school could now issue bachelor of religious education degrees. The association approved the proposal and the name changed in 1971.

The following reasons were given for changing the name in the Winter 1971 *R.B.I. Newsletter*:

1. Because of our four-year Bachelor of religious education degree course, the name "college" more accurately reflects that academic character, education level, and purpose of the school—an important factor in student recruitment and public relations.

2. Because member schools of the Accrediting Association of Bible Colleges which offer four-year degree programs use the name "college."

3. Because the name "institute" in some states and foreign countries signifies an education level below or different from that of a degree-granting college.

Though the school expanded its degree offerings and changed its name, school leaders continued to emphasize the difference between a "liberal arts" college and a Bible college. "As Christians, we are grateful for both types of schools," noted President Van Halsema in the Spring 1972 newsletter. "Many young people with a sense of divine calling for congregational, evangelistic, and missionary work (in a capacity other than ordained) choose the Bible college."

Enrollment immediately swelled, and for the first time RBI had four classes of students and a recognized academic degree. Tuition was increased to $300 per semester with room and board costing $440 per semester. The first three BRE degrees were handed out on June 3, 1971.

In subsequent years, permission was also granted for a two-year associate in religious education degree, a one-year diploma and a one-year certificate of biblical studies, and also a master of religious education degree.

*Chris wrote these memories in 2009. She is a job coach at Kandu Inc. in Holland, Michigan, a not-for-profit organization focused on building work skills and creating opportunities for people with barriers to employment.*

What I remember most about my journey through RBC was probably the life-changing effect that it had on me. Coming out of high school from a little farm in South Dakota to the big city life of Grand Rapids was a big step. My leadership skills were developed while I was at RBC through the challenges of the classroom. In keeping with the mission statement that has always been constant through RBI, RBC, and Kuyper, they trained me to walk into ministry. And it wasn't just classroom teaching.

Throughout the years the College has been faithful to God's Word and faithful to the Jesus model of making disciples. There I was equipped to do that, and it's been pretty much a part of my life and my career—walking with people and equipping them to be grounded in God's Word.

What I see at Kuyper today is an expansion of academic programs that give students broader educational options and different ways to serve in Christ's kingdom. However, what impresses me the most is that I see the same thing that brought me here in 1973—the solid foundation that does not change because it is non-negotiable—it is a constant.

In 1971, the Reformed Bible Institute became the Reformed Bible College to better reflect the school's status as a four-year-degree-granting college.

## Faculty and Staff Developments and Course Expansion

After the challenges faced in the late 1960s, the years from 1970 to 1980 were years of significant academic expansion. Critical self-evaluations of the school's curriculum, teaching methods, and organizational structure were conducted. As a result, faculty members were added to the staff to teach English, speech, history, communications, sociology, social work, Greek, Spanish, and more.

The decade was also marked by changes in the faculty and staff. Sarah Fredricks, who served as the secretary to the president, worked at the school following her graduation in 1942 until her retirement in 1972. In 1973, Rev. John H. Schaal retired and in 1978, Katie Gunnink retired. Dr. Lubbertus Oostendorp, who had served as RBC's professor of theology since 1964, retired in 1979.

Many long-serving faculty and staff members were hired during this formative decade who taught a full range of subjects leading to BRE and ARE degrees as well as the certificate of biblical studies.

- William (Bill) Jansen became the business manager in 1971. Later he served as the vice president for stewardship and became known as "Mr. RBC" to donors.

- Thea Van Halsema, President Van Halsema's wife, joined the faculty in 1972 as a social work instructor. She also served as dean of women.
- Dr. James Ritsema was appointed in 1973 as the school's first Christian service director to help supervise students' field assignments.
- Rev. George Kroeze was appointed in 1974 as a Bible professor. He was the first non-Christian Reformed Church faculty member (he was a member of the Reformed Church in America).
- Nelle Vander Ark taught Bible, English, and education courses beginning in 1975.
- Dr. Paul Bremer was hired in 1975 to teach Greek, biblical studies, and philosophy.
- Dr. Burt Braunius, an RBI alumnus, became Katie Gunnink's successor in 1976 and taught church education.

- Dan Bloem joined the staff of RBC in 1978 to establish a public relations department.
- Rev. William Shell was hired in 1979 as a Bible professor.
- Dr. J. Dudley Woodberry, an expert in Islamic studies and Islamic-Christian relations, was added to the missions department in 1979. He later joined the faculty of Fuller Theological Seminary.

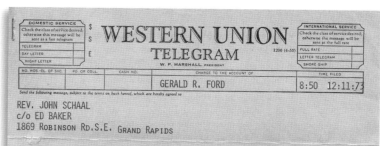

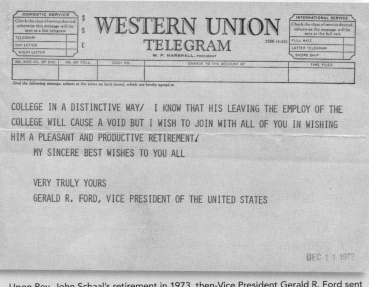

DEAR MR. BAKER: I UNDERSTAND THAT YOU AND OTHERS ARE ASSEMBLED THIS FRIDAY IN HONOR OF THE REV. JOHN SCHAAL, ONE WHO HAS GIVEN UNSTINTINGLY OF HIMSELF FOR 25 YEARS TO THE REFORMED BIBLE COLLEGE/ I HAVE KNOWN THE REV. SCHAAL PERSONALLY FOR A NUMBER OF YEARS AND HAVE ALSO HAD THE PLEASURE OF ATTENDING SOME PAST PRESIDENTIAL PRAYER BREAKFASTS WITH HIM/ HE AND MY FORMER ADMIN-ISTRATIVE ASSISTANT, THE LATE FRANK MEYER, WERE ALSO VERY CLOSE// AT THE TIME OF FRANK"S PASSING ON I FOUND THE REV. SCHAAL TO BE A VERY WELCOME PIL-LAR OF STRENGTH/ I AM CERTAIN THAT HE HAS ALSO SERVED THE REFORMED BIBLE

COLLEGE IN A DISTINCTIVE WAY/ I KNOW THAT HIS LEAVING THE EMPLOY OF THE COLLEGE WILL CAUSE A VOID BUT I WISH TO JOIN WITH ALL OF YOU IN WISHING HIM A PLEASANT AND PRODUCTIVE RETIREMENT/
    MY SINCERE BEST WISHES TO YOU ALL

    VERY TRULY YOURS
    GERALD R. FORD, VICE PRESIDENT OF THE UNITED STATES

DEC 11 1973

Many commencement ceremonies were held at Calvin Christian Reformed Church, where President Van Halsema and his wife were members. Pictured is the 1973 ceremony.

Upon Rev. John Schaal's retirement in 1973, then-Vice President Gerald R. Ford sent a congratulatory telegram honoring him. Schaal and Ford were personal friends for many years.

The faculty for the 1972–1973 school year is pictured here. First row (left to right): Katie Gunnink, Rev. John Schaal, Dr. Dick Van Halsema, Harold Bruxvoort, and Joanne Boehm. Second row: Lubbertus Oostendorp, Jack Van Laar, Addison Soltau, Eugene Ver Hage, and Dr. James Ritsema.

Rev. George Kroeze was the chairman of the board in the 1970s and became a full-time faculty member in 1974. Students recall when Professor Kroeze was teaching and stood on his toes, he was saying something very important that they should remember for an exam.

The faculty of the 1975–1976 school year included (left to right) Dr. George Kroeze, Dr. Lubbertus Oostendorp, Dr. James Ritsema, Eugene Ver Hage, and Dr. Paul Bremer.

Johanna Timmer, the first instructor of the school, returned to RBC in 1977, a year before her death, when the main building at the 1869 Robinson Road campus was named "Timmer Hall" in her honor. She is pictured here with Calvin Bolt (board chairman) and Sarah Fredricks (1942 graduate and secretary to the president).

By 1980, the faculty included seventeen full-time and twelve part-time employees. Other people not listed here served the school faithfully throughout the years, fulfilling God's calling on their lives to teach and minister to students at the Reformed Bible College.

## Further Campus Expansion

With the implementation of the four-year program, other needs became apparent: faculty expansion, curriculum development, administrative revision, staff strengthening, and—yet again—campus enlargement. In March 1973, the board approved three new building projects under the leadership of Rev. George Kroeze, chairman of the board and later a faculty member. The first project, a library and classroom addition, was ready for use in the fall of 1974. The $240,000 cost was greatly offset by an anonymous donation of $100,000 from a west Michigan family foundation.

In 1976, Rev. John Schaal broke ground for a residence hall that would bear his name. The building, which was built to house seventy-two students, was completed in 1977 at a cost of $320,000.

THE WHITE HOUSE
WASHINGTON

January 5, 1977

Dear Mr. Van Halsema:

My warmest congratulations to all those who have had a part in the dedication of the first dormitory facility on the campus of the Reformed Bible College in Grand Rapids.

This is an important step forward in strengthening the dynamic spiritual and moral leadership by which this fine institution so effectively serves the well-being of our hometown.

I welcome this opportunity to express my warmest regards to my good and longtime friend, Dean John Schaal, and to extend my very best wishes to you and those who will continue to guide the progress and development of the College in the years ahead.

Sincerely,

Gerald R. Ford

Mr. Richard Van Halsema
President
Reformed Bible College
1869 Robinson Road
Grand Rapids, Michigan 49506

This 1977 letter from President Gerald R. Ford to RBC President Dick Van Halsema congratulates the school on the completion of Schaal Hall. President Ford was a "good and long-time friend" of Rev. John Schaal.

In 1973, the board approved three construction projects, including a library and classroom wing. Ground was broken in February and the new wing was completed at a cost of $240,000 before the end of the year.

By October 1974, the $240,000 cost of the new addition was entirely paid off.

The Walters Campus Center was the last of three large building projects completed in the 1970s. Ground was broken on November 3, 1977.

The next building project, a residence hall, was completed in January 1977 at a cost of $320,000. Designed to house seventy-two students, it was named Schaal Hall in honor of board member, dean, and faculty member John Schaal, who retired in 1973 after more than twenty-five years of service to the school.

The third and final building project completed in a four-year timespan was the Walters Campus Center, which was completed in 1978. Named for the college's first president, Dick H. Walters, the building became the largest structure on campus and included a food service complex on the second floor and a student recreation room, lounge, business and accounting offices, bookstore, and special purpose rooms on the first floor.

In the late 1970s, the board reaffirmed for the third time in about ten years that the college should remain at the Robinson Road campus location. With that in mind, nearby

The ribbon-cutting ceremony (1978) for the Walters Campus Center was attended by the Walters family who are pictured here with Food Service Manager Clare Hempel (second from right) and Business Manager Bill Jansen (right).

During the 1960s and 1970s, the college expanded the physical boundaries of its campus by purchasing adjacent houses that were then used as dormitories. Pictured is West Hall in 1981.

Though the Reformed Bible College desired to expand its facilities, neighbors wanted to maintain the residential feel of the neighborhood and they mounted opposition to RBC's plans as this *Grand Rapids Press* article from December 29, 1981, shows.

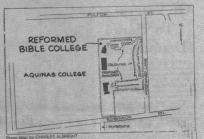
residential properties were purchased to complement the parcels acquired in the late 1960s. With the exception of one Woodward Lane property, RBC's campus ran from Robinson Road north to Fulton Street with Woodward Lane as the east boundary and the Aquinas College campus as the boundary on the west.

In 1979, a second long-range campus development plan was created. The hope was that four new structures would be constructed on the Robinson Road campus: a field house/physical education facility, a library, and two additional housing units. However, opposition arose from neighbors and the Grand Rapids City Planning Commission blocked plans for the field house in the years to follow.

The Women's Fellowship of the Reformed Bible College were supporters of the college who met regularly for prayer and to address various needs of the institution and its students. The women pictured above are some of the members of that group.

This development would delay the process of expanding the campus and providing facilities to meet the needs of the college as it grew.

## The RBC Women's Fellowship and Campus Events

A women's fellowship was formed early in the school's history to support the school in prayer, to organize various groups and fundraisers, and to aid the school materially in any way they could. The fellowship was open to students, staff, and interested members of the community with meetings held every third Monday of the month.

One popular event the RBC Women's Fellowship held began as a "Coffee Klets" on campus at the first RBC public auction in May 1971. By 1973, the auction became the annual International Harvest Festival, a popular fundraiser for the school. Colorful booths displayed wares from international students' countries from around the world that were available for purchase. The Women's Fellowship, alumni, staff, faculty, and board all worked together to make meals, donate items, work in booths, greet visitors, and more.

The income received from this yearly event went to special projects around the college;

The college used promotional displays, like the one pictured above at a Fall Festival in 1978, to advertise its purpose and mission.

This Southeast Asia table, staffed by students, shows items from Nepal at the 1982 Fall Festival. RBC's Fall Festival (formerly called the International Harvest Festival) was an annual event that began in the 1970s.

# Anniversary Bibles

Since God's Word was central to academic life at the Reformed Bible College, it seemed only natural that the institution would have a role in distributing Bibles. The college developed a tradition of giving away Bibles for a number of its anniversaries and to commemorate other special occasions. In 1965, the college gave out 2,500 Bibles for its twenty-fifth anniversary, and the tradition continued through the school's fiftieth anniversary. RBC gave other Bibles to various Christian Reformed mission teams and groups.

This endeavor was helped greatly by Pat Zondervan, one of the founding board members of the Reformed Bible Institute and one of the two founders of Zondervan® Publishers. Today, the Zondervan Library on campus is named after him. The library is a repository for the publishing company and receives a copy of each book and Bible published by them.

RBC developed a tradition of anniversary dinners that became very popular in the 1970s. This picture is of the 1977 dinner held at the Welsh Civic Auditorium. Later the events were called the Annual Gala.

The food service staff is pictured here in 1981 with Food Service Director Clare Hempel (far left), who served at the school from 1975 through the 1990s.

Jonas Chupp ('61 and '75), director of maintenance, is pictured in 1983 loading a station wagon donated to the college by the Women's Fellowship.

Students took an active part in various dimensions of college life. The students pictured above in 1975 in the new library were a part of the Library Committee.

for example, the $5,000 raised in 1976 was earmarked for drapes and bedspreads for Schaal Hall. Other funds were used for various student needs: winter clothing for international students, dental bills, groceries for student families, and more.

Another significant source of income for the school came from annual Anniversary Dinners that began in the 1970s. One of the first of these popular events was held in 1974 at the Grand Valley National Guard Armory in Wyoming, Michigan, and attracted seven hundred guests. When the armory became too small, the event moved to the Welsh Civic Auditorium and later to the Gerald R. Ford Fieldhouse and attracted as many as

1,200 guests. Though the banquets would change in their nature through the years, they continue to be a part of the history of the college and a significant element in raising awareness and financial support for the college.

## Student Life

Great effort was made during these years to maintain and promote a unique place of fellowship characterized by a love for the Lord, a hunger for His Word, and a desire to serve Him better. Chapel services were held daily and were well attended and much appreciated. Students, faculty members,

Many students participated in school-sponsored extracurricular activities like Student Council, pictured here in 1978. Rev. George Kroeze (eighth from left) was the advisor.

and guests shared messages from the Bible. Prayer meetings were regularly scheduled but also held voluntarily in classrooms and dormitories. But it was also a time period characterized by change.

"The decade of the 1970s began with RBI women students wearing the first mini-skirts on campus. A couple of years later, they came in slacks...came jeans and overalls," recalled faculty member Katie Gunnink. "Faculty discussions about a dress code were held... The days of the well-dressed student was over. Students wanted freedom and informality in dress, candor and openness in class discussions, and authenticity in Christian life and conversation."

Though the clothing and manner of learning had changed, the purpose of the

Reformed Bible College and the desires of students and faculty to serve the Lord remained steadfast. "One of the greatest joys for faculty members always has been to see students' lives transformed under the teaching of God's Word...In a genuine sense, students who 'with unveiled faces' gazed into the mirror of God's Word saw the glory of the Lord in the face of Jesus. Inevitably they became transformed into that image, and they never again were the same," noted Gunnink. "After such exposure, they made lifelong commitments to serve the Lord in churches, missions, and daily vocations throughout the world."

The library staff of students was led for many years by Joanne Boehm (in the striped dress).

Though official sports teams were not a part of college life until 2006, in earlier years students often formed teams and scheduled games with area organizations on their own. Here the 1980 soccer team poses for a picture.

*Chapter 6*

# Continued Developments and Changes: 1980–1988

In its fifth decade of service to God and His Kingdom, the original purpose of the Reformed Bible College continued to shine through: to know Christ and make Him known. The school, after a decade filled with growth and change, now had solid footing on which to stand. Enrollment reached a record level of 240 students, and academic programs spanned the entire year.

Support of RBC was also widespread. Churches were now regularly looking for RBC graduates to staff their churches and go out on the mission field. Many successful anniversary dinners were held as fundraisers, and many churches from more than just the Christian Reformed denomination were committed to supporting RBC financially.

Because of the financial support from individuals and churches, tuition at RBC remained competitive with other colleges in the United States. In 1981, tuition was set at $2,120 for the entire year. With housing and books, the total cost estimate was $4,200 annually. National studies at that time showed the average annual cost of private colleges was $6,885, while public colleges had an average annual cost of $3,873.

Because of the record enrollment and solid financial footing the school was on, it became necessary once again to expand both physically and academically. Plans for a gymnasium and assembly building were drawn up. School leaders also began to explore the possibility of implementing a master of religious education degree for missionaries and pastors. The Lord continued to abundantly bless the works of the Reformed Bible College.

## RBC Offers Four Majors

By 1984, the Reformed Bible College offered four major subject areas for students. Each student was expected to major in biblical/theological studies and could also choose one additional major if they desired. The three other majors offered were evangelism/missions, Christian education, and music.

The biblical/theological studies major required students to earn thirty-nine credit hours in biblical introduction, Reformed doctrine, the study of various books of the Bible, and other related courses.

The classroom and chapel addition built in 1958 served the college well through the 1980s until the college relocated.

The evangelism/missions major focused on pastoral leadership development, evangelistic preaching, and basic Bible teaching. Many students in this program participated in the Summer Training Session offered by RBC to learn more about cross-cultural mission work.

Male dormitory residents pose in front of the Geneva Hall dormitory in 1981.

The Christian education major trained students to be effective educators. "In today's Christian church there is a great need for staff members who have an unwavering conviction, a reproducing faith, a creative mindset, and a dynamic, hopeful vision of God's kingdom," noted RBC graduate Paul Burmeister (1984) in the Fall 1984 newsletter.

The music major taught students how to lead worship and hone their musical abilities. The major required twenty-one credit hours of music classes and three credit hours of private lessons or ensemble. A fifteen-credit music minor was also available.

Along with the required biblical/theological studies major, students were also required to complete courses for a communications minor. Students took five liberal arts courses: English Composition, Principles of Public Speaking, Principles of Journalism, Survey of American Literature, and Literary Classics.

Faculty and staff members regularly joined students in worship in chapel every Monday, Wednesday, and Friday. Pictured here in 1984 (left to right) are Dr. Lyle Bierma, Tom Holwerda, Harold Bruxvoort, Dr. George Kroeze, Dr. Burt Braunius, and Dr. Paul Bremer.

Dormitory residents pose in front of Schaal Hall in 1985.

## Master of Religious Education Degree

In addition to the bachelor in religious education degree, in January 1986 RBC began offering a master of religious education (MRE). The degree was offered to those with at least two years of full-time ministry experience who wished to further their education beyond a traditional undergraduate degree. Students could earn the degree in two semesters (with fifteen credit hours earned in each) if they had already completed a bachelor's degree and other prerequisite requirements.

After the program launched, only a few students pursued the MRE. Shortly after it began, the program ended.

North Hall residents pose on the stairway of the dormitory in 1985.

The small library on the 1869 Robinson Road campus was the site of many long study sessions. Though the college made plans to build a new library, opposition arose from neighbors who desired to preserve the residential feel of the neighborhood.

## Attempts to Expand College Facilities

During the late 1970s, plans were drawn up for further development of the Robinson Road campus. The main project planned was a gymnasium and assembly building and was generously supported by a large gift given in 1980 by Mike and Lillian Boonstra, but a library and two housing units were also planned. In 1983, the school purchased two residential properties, one on Woodward Lane and one on Fulton Street, paving the way for these projects to begin.

However, despite solid financial support and approval from the board for the project, opposition would soon arise. Neighbors objected to the planned expansion and formed the Woodward Lane Association to stop the project. They lobbied (at the Grand Rapids City Planning Commission) to block RBC's approval for the building plans from 1980 to 1982. These objections, along with an economic recession in the United States and a tapering off of student enrollment at the college, lessened the urgency for campus expansion.

One positive result of the neighbors' opposition was RBC's efforts to cultivate better relationships with them. A series of informal luncheons and dinner meetings were held on and off campus with neighbors, students, faculty, and staff. Finally, in the spring of 1987, Woodward Lane Association representatives agreed they would have no objection to a new library building on RBC's campus.

## Faculty and Staff Development

The 1970s was a decade filled with new full-time faculty and staff members, and the trend continued into the 1980s.

- In 1980, Dr. Lyle Bierma was appointed a theology professor.
- Kenneth Bos was appointed in 1980 to the music department.
- Dr. Richard Hertel began work at RBC in 1983 as a missions and evangelism professor.
- In 1986, Pat Tigchelaar was appointed as a communications professor.
- In 1987, Dianne Zandbergen became the director of library sciences. She is still working in that position in the Zondervan Library today.

Nelle Vander Ark served as a professor of communications from 1975 to 1986. In addition to her work at the college, she became a popular Bible study teacher in area churches.

Director of Maintenance Jonas Chupp (right), pictured here in 1982 with student workers, was hired in 1965 and served for more than twenty-five years. His son, Tim Chupp, is the current maintenance director at the college.

Board members in 1987 accepted the retirement of President Dick L. Van Halsema and appointed Dr. Edwin D. Roels as the next president. Van Halsema is pictured on the bottom row, third from the right. Pictured in the top row (left) is Dan Vos, who played a critical role in the design and construction of the new campus.

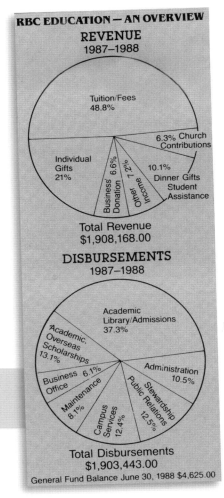

**RBC EDUCATION — AN OVERVIEW**

**REVENUE**
1987–1988

Tuition/Fees
48.8%

6.3% Church
Contributions

Individual
Gifts
21%

Business
Donation 6.6%

Other
Income 7.2%

10.1%
Dinner Gifts
Student
Assistance

Total Revenue
$1,908,168.00

**DISBURSEMENTS**
1987–1988

Academic
Library/Admissions
37.3%

Academic,
Overseas
Scholarships
13.1%

Business
Office 6.1%

Maintenance
8.1%

Campus
Services
12.4%

Stewardship
Public Relations
12.5%

Administration
10.5%

Total Disbursements
$1,903,443.00
General Fund Balance June 30, 1988 $4,625.00

These pie charts from the 1987–1988 school year reflect the college's revenue sources and disbursement.

## Dr. Edwin D. Roels Becomes the Third President

On July 31, 1987, President Van Halsema retired, which meant the third president of the college would need to be found. The board selected Dr. Edwin D. Roels who began his term as president on August 1. Dr. Roels previously served as the pastor of Unity Christian Reformed Church in Prinsburg, Minnesota, and had formerly worked at Calvin College and Trinity College in Illinois. Dr. Roels and his family also served in Korea from 1967 to 1970 at the American Home for Servicemen through the Christian Reformed Board of Home Missions.

At the beginning of his time at the Reformed Bible College, Dr. Roels penned an article in the Fall 1987 *RBC Newsletter* acknowledging the rich history of the institution. "It's encouraging for me personally to know that the foundation on which we built here is solid and firm, carefully put in place by a multitude of faithful and dedicated servants who have preceded me," he wrote.

Dr. Edwin D. Roels became the third president of RBC in 1987. He is pictured here in the president's office in Timmer Hall on the Robinson Road campus. Dr. Roels retired in 1995.

During his years of service, Dr. Roels would carefully guide the college through several important transitions, including the move to a new campus and the accreditation the school received in 1995 from the North Central Association.

## Conversations Begin with Aquinas College

During his first year as president, Dr. Roels was invited to get acquainted with the president of the neighboring Aquinas College, Dr. Peter O'Connor. Over lunch, O'Connor reviewed each institution's history of expansion difficulties. RBC needed more facilities including a library, field house, and dormitories, and Aquinas also needed more dormitory and classroom space.

In the course of the conversation, O'Connor remarked that one obvious solution would be if one school would

purchase the other school's property. This solution would solve both schools' problems: one school could expand onto the other school's site and the other school would be able to relocate to a more adequate site.

In prior years, RBC and Aquinas College had informal conversations about better utilization of their campuses and realized both needed additional space for development. But prior to this conversation between Dr. O'Connor and Dr. Roels, the conversations would take place and then be discontinued. Now, the timing was finally right to continue the discussion.

A committee was then formed with representatives from both RBC and Aquinas to explore whether a property sale would be a viable option considering both institutions' long-term growth plans. Since the Aquinas property was sixty acres and the RBC property was seventeen acres, the most obvious exchange would be that Aquinas

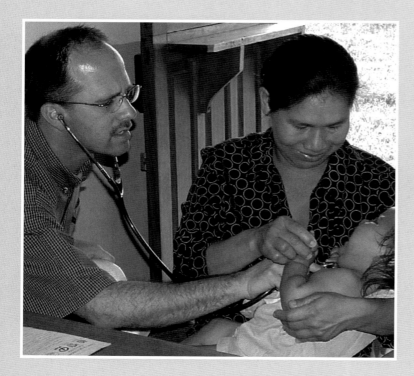

"Where we live there was no electricity and no running water for years. A local church in Michigan provided the funds for us to dig a well and once we got a generator, another provided a pump. It is the only way for us to get fresh water. Up until then we consumed the village's water which comes from a mountain on a gravity system. It is very dirty, and sometimes there are water blockages because large snakes—boas—get caught in the ducts."

That is how Rick Lampen (1986) describes the almost primitive conditions of the village of Yotau, on the edge of the Bolivian jungle, where he currently serves as a medical missionary. Yotau, south of the Amazon Basin, has but a few red dirt streets and a population just over one hundred.

Lampen grew up in Zeeland, Michigan. Upon his return home from a high school mission trip, he felt the need to attend a college that provided Bible training but also had an emphasis on missions. "The Lord opened up the door—RBC had exactly what I was looking for. I graduated with a Bachelor in Religious Education."

According to Lampen, RBC's professors encouraged all the students to grow and develop their faith. "It was there that I was able to develop the skills and abilities that prepared me for the mission field. All of that and the prayer groups on campus helped us become more aware of the needs around the world. The Lord really used my time at the College to change my life, sanctifying it to His kingdom work. It prepared me for what I needed in missions."

After graduation, Lampen attended Indiana Wesleyan University where he received a bachelor in nursing degree and met his wife Lori, also a nursing student. Today, Rick, Lori, and their daughter Kaylinn serve as missionaries in Bolivia. On average, he sees between 200 and 250 patients monthly from Yotau and neighboring villages. Besides running their clinic and sharing God's Word with patients there, Rick and Lori are involved in youth ministries and teach classes to new believers in their small church.

would purchase RBC's property and RBC would relocate.

One of the board members of RBC on the committee was Daniel R. Vos, president of Dan Vos Construction Company. Vos, experienced in commercial construction, provided valuable insight into the value of RBC's current campus and the cost to replace it at a new location.

After lengthy negotiations, Aquinas College and Reformed Bible College agreed on a sale price of $6 million for the RBC campus with payments made in equal installments over ten years. The terms of sale were finalized on July 12, 1988, and included eleven buildings on seventeen acres of land. Reformed Bible College was given two years to find a new location and vacate the current campus.

Dr. Roels, in a July 13 press release, remarked, "The Reformed Bible College staff and board have sensed the leading of God in a special way over the past several months and joyfully anticipate the future development of our college in a new location."

Purchased in 1947, the Robinson Road campus had served the Reformed Bible College well for more than forty years, but the time had come to move.

On November 11, 1988, the final papers for the sale of the Robinson Road campus were signed by RBC President Roels (second from left) and Aquinas College President Dr. Peter O'Connor (second from right). RBC Board Secretary John Huff is on the left.

## Chapter 7

# Relocation and Broader Accreditation: 1988–1995

After forty years of education and ministry at the Robinson Road campus in Grand Rapids, the time had come for Reformed Bible College to relocate. "As we make our plans for the future, we do so with thoughtfulness and prayer, but also with anticipation and joy—confident that God is truly leading us every step of the way," wrote President Roels in the Fall 1988 newsletter.

The time of the move seemed opportune for a number of reasons. First, the school had outgrown its current campus. Existing buildings were being used for purposes for which they were not intended, and new buildings needed to be erected to meet the growing needs of the school—buildings that would be very costly. The sale of the campus offered a fresh slate from which to start, and furthermore, the funds from the sale would greatly help defray the costs to build the new campus.

Another beneficial and economical reason for the move to a new campus was maintenance costs at the current campus had risen dramatically in the past decade. With newer buildings on a new campus, maintenance costs would be less. It would also be easier to build on a new campus without opposition from neighbors of the Robinson Road campus who desired to maintain the residential feel of their neighborhood.

A third financial reason for the campus move was donors would be more excited to help build it from the ground up rather than renovating the buildings on the former campus. The college's fiftieth anniversary was quickly approaching, and it was a good time to energize alumni and supporters from around the world for this new endeavor.

The Reformed Bible College's impending move would pave the way for new growth. "As we approach the twenty-first century, we hope to create a powerful new vision for ministry...one which reflects our goals for the future while retaining the strengths and traditions of the past," stated Roels.

## Finding a New Location

After the sale of the Robinson Road campus to Aquinas came the unique challenge of having to find a suitable location for a new campus. Several important factors were considered such as space for future growth, accessibility for students and the general community, proximity to other educational institutions, and price.

More than twenty possible locations were considered of less than ten acres to more than one hundred acres. There was broad support for keeping the school in Grand Rapids so the search was focused on finding a site within the city or in the larger Grand Rapids area.

In the midst of these relocating decisions, Sunshine Christian Reformed Church (now Sunshine Community Church) on the edge of Grand Rapids contacted college

Geeta (Grace) Mondol (1991) grew up in a conservative Hindu family in Kanpur, India. During her grade school years, she began to have serious questions about her family's Hindu faith. After graduating from high school, her search for God intensified and she eventually came to know Christ through the witness of Christians at her college in New Delhi.

But the years after her conversion were very challenging times and the relationship with her family was strained. When Geeta was baptized, her parents arranged a marriage with a Hindu man Geeta had never met. She immediately went into hiding with nothing more than her Bible and the clothes on her back and eventually fled to the United States.

While in the United States, she received the news that the Reformed Bible College was willing to give her an International Student Scholarship. Two years later, Geeta graduated from the college with a bachelor of religious education degree.

Geeta returned to India after her graduation from RBC, reconciled with her parents, married, and had two sons. Her oldest son was diagnosed with high-functioning autism and the news started Geeta on a journey. After starting a special needs program in her son's school, Geeta felt led to begin a biblically based program for children with special needs called the Ashish Centre (ashish means blessing) to provide intervention as well as training and counseling for parents.

The Ashish Centre opened its doors in April 2007 and now serves thirty-eight students, aged three to twenty-five. Besides the Ashish Centre, Geeta heads a community project serving children from very poor families and helps mentally challenged, destitute women receive vocational education and other therapies.

Geeta Mondol (second from left) and her family live in New Delhi, India.

The agreement for RBC to purchase the Sunshine Christian Reformed Church property was signed on December 15, 1988, by Sunshine Board Member Larry Fredericks (left) and RBC President Dr. Edwin Roels (right).

representatives with a suggestion. The church was in the process of building a new complex across from the site of their current church building and wished to sell RBC the seventeen-acre site and current 20,000-square-foot church building along with the surrounding pine forests.

The property bordered the two-lane East Beltline road and also included emergency access onto Bird Avenue on the west side of the property. Plans were in place to upgrade the East Beltline road into a divided roadway with two lanes in each direction, enhancing accessibility to the site.

However, the Reformed Bible College had just sold the seventeen-acre Robinson Road property and desired more than seventeen acres for long-range growth. Leaders at Sunshine Church, after hearing this concern, asked for one week to come up with another proposal for the property. One week later, church representatives offered a twenty-nine-

## NEW BEGINNINGS

This artist's rendering shows the third-floor entryway and atrium of the new library and classroom building.

This artist's rendering of the third-floor entrance shows the final design selected for the new academic building. The two-story Zondervan Library is on the left.

This master plan of the new campus of the college was created to span several construction "phases." The first phase did not originally include plans for a freestanding chapel.

RBC President Ed Roels spoke at a groundbreaking ceremony on the site of the new campus in 1989. The existing building in the background was renovated for $551,793 into a student center connected by a covered walkway to the chapel.

acre parcel: the seventeen previously offered acres along with twelve additional acres on the north side of the property upon which sat a home and orchard.

Next to be negotiated was the cost. One Sunshine Church member commented, "I don't care if R.B.C. is offering us $50 for the whole business; I feel that we should work with them so as to keep the property with a church agency." Though somewhat humorously stated, the tone of the negotiations was friendly and cooperative between RBC and Sunshine.

After extensive deliberation and discussion, the Reformed Bible College Board agreed to purchase the twenty-nine-acre property for a total of $1,100,000. RBC signed the buy/sell agreement for the property at 3295 East Beltline in late 1988. The address would later be changed to 3333 East Beltline NE.

## Building the New Campus

The next step for the Reformed Bible College would be determining how to best develop the new property to meet the school's needs. The board selected Dan Vos, a fellow board member, to oversee the design/build process. Dan Vos Construction Company had a good reputation for well-built church and commercial buildings throughout west Michigan. As a board member, Vos understood the college and its distinctives.

Vos soon developed a sketch of interconnected buildings with a 250-seat semicircular chapel as its center point with hallways radiating out from it. The design tied in the already-present building as a student center.

However, the board expressed some concern about the timing and cost of the proposed design. In the tradition of conservative fiscal policy, they desired each

# Legacy of Dan Vos

*The entire article first appeared in the* Grand Rapids Press *on Friday, October 12, 1990.*

A proud papa's smile came to Dan Vos' face as the strains of the hymn "I Will Extol You, O My God" resounded inside the just-completed chapel on the new campus of the Reformed Bible College.

The hymn was the first song ever sung in the place of worship that Vos himself envisioned, helped design, and paid more than $700,000 to create. Named after him, the chapel caps a career in which he has constructed more than 100 churches throughout West Michigan.

"The concept for this chapel is mine 100 percent," said Vos, retired president of Dan Vos Construction Co. "This is my final project, I swear to that. It feels real good to end my career with this."

The octagonal-shaped chapel is one of five buildings Vos helped design and construct on the campus, which sits on 29 acres along East Beltline north of Three Mile Road NW.

A three-story administration and library building, a renovated student center, an apartment building and dormitory also comprise the campus of the school.

"I've always had great respect for this institution," said Vos, who lives in Ada. "The first $20 I ever put in a collection plate was for the Reformed Bible College."

Board Member Dan Vos (left), with President Roels, is pictured in the octagonal chapel his company, Dan Vos Construction, designed and was donated by the Vos family.

The Dan Vos Construction Company designed the new campus to take advantage of the rolling terrain of the new property on East Beltline. When construction was finished, the main entrances were on the third floor at one side of the building and on the first floor at the other side of the building.

The bulk of the new campus construction was done in 1989.

Timmer Hall, a dormitory on the new campus, was constructed in 1989 at a cost of $872,713.

building's cost be pledged or underwritten prior to construction. This presented a challenge, as there were several buildings that were urgently needed, like classroom space, administrative offices, a library, food service, and student housing.

As the board looked at the Vos plans, they felt the construction would need to happen in phases and the chapel would have to wait.

The first phase would add a food service area to the existing building on the property and new construction would include the library and education building along with dormitories. The second phase would be the construction of a fitness center and married housing, and the third phase—down the road—would include additional housing and possibly a mission training center.

The new three-story academic building was completed in 1990. The cost for this building was $4,773,713.

Construction on the academic building included an entrance on the third floor. The arched window pictured is located in the Zondervan Room.

The new campus of the Reformed Bible College was completed and ready for use in June 1990. Shortly after construction was completed on the college, the East Beltline was upgraded into a four-lane roadway with a median.

The Zondervan Library is a popular place for students to gather and study.

Ground was broken for the new Boonstra Fitness Center in 1992 thanks to funds donated by Mike and Lillian Boonstra. Lillian Boonstra is pictured on the right next to President Ed Roels.

The Holt Apartments are named after Ken and June Holtvluwer and were completed during the main phase of construction. Seven total apartments (and a laundry room) could house thirty-five total students.

As plans were made, many donors of gifts, large and small, came forward. Board member Dan R. Vos donated the funds for the chapel as part of the first phase of construction, and founding board member Pat J. Zondervan (co-founder of Zondervan® Publishers) and his wife Mary underwrote the cost of the library. William and Martha DeWitt supported the student center renovations, and Ken and June Holtvluwer funded the Holt Apartments. Later, the Boonstra Fitness Center would be built using funds donated by Mike and Lillian Boonstra.

The total cost of the new campus would come to $9,605,800, which included the cost of the property. A total of $4,773,713 was spent on the library/office/classroom building (including design), $872,713 was spent building the Timmer Hall dormitory, $592,649 was spent on an apartment building, $551,793 was used to renovate the existing building into a student center, and $738,274 was spent on the chapel. In addition, $898,000 was used on equipment and furnishings.

The May 1989 graduation ceremony was held in the vacant Sunshine Church building on the new campus. During the ceremony, the college broke ground on the construction of the new campus. After twenty-four months of construction, staff and faculty made the move to the new campus at 3333 East Beltline in June 1990.

Through the whole process of selling the old campus, selecting a new location, and constructing the new campus, the heart and mission of the Reformed Bible College remained faithful. "Ministry has always been the center of attention at R.B.C. And it must always be," emphasized President Roels. "A new campus, no matter how beautiful, is of no value without ministry. If we did not sincerely believe that we can serve the Lord more effectively by moving to a new campus, we would not move. It's as simple as that."

# Artwork for the
# New Campus

While the new campus was being constructed, a few people suggested the college acquire some pieces of art that would highlight the school's religious focus and mission. A modest budget was provided and a team of faculty and board members approached artists, many from the Grand Rapids community, and made purchases and received gifts to acquire the collection.

- Eunice Bolt

  *Beside Still Waters*

- Edgar Boevé: four scenes that depict Jesus' instructions to his followers

  *Go, Be Fishers of Men*

  *Go, Feed My Sheep*

  *Go, Feed My Flock*

  *Go, Bring the Harvest*

- Chris Overvoorde: six depictions of events from the Old Testament

  *Ahimelech Priest; the Bread of Life*

  *Aaron; One Scapegoat for All*

  *Moses; Was Called*

  *Jeremiah; Down, Deep Down*

  *Ezra; Message from Watergate*

  *Eli; Highpriest; Helpless Father*

- Tim Van Laar: a scene which contrasts the Tower of Babel where languages became divided and confused and Pentecost where the disciples were able to speak in many languages

  *Babble/Tongues*

- Pat Verduin

  *Living Cross*

- John Swanson

  *Ecclesiastes*

  *Celebration*

  *The Shepherds*

  *The Epiphany*

  *Nativity*

Other various rugs and wall hangings adorn the hallways of the college, including the piece *Angkor Wok* given to the college by a student from Cambodia, whose family had smuggled the artwork out of the country when they fled from Cambodia. Fold marks in the artwork are visible from when the piece was taken from the country to the United States.

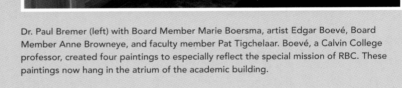

Dr. Paul Bremer (left) with Board Member Marie Boersma, artist Edgar Boevé, Board Member Anne Browneye, and faculty member Pat Tigchelaar. Boevé, a Calvin College professor, created four paintings to especially reflect the special mission of RBC. These paintings now hang in the atrium of the academic building.

## Collaboration with Other Colleges

Over the years on its new campus, RBC worked with several other colleges to expand course and degree offerings. In 1994, RBC and Cornerstone College (now Cornerstone University) announced a cooperative program for students who wanted to be teachers. The move gave RBC students an expanded course offering beyond that which RBC offered.

Students in the collaborative program studied for three years at RBC followed by two years of study at Cornerstone. Since Cornerstone's campus was located just three miles south of RBC's campus on the East Beltline road, students didn't have to travel far to take classes at either school. Graduates received two degrees: a bachelor in religious education from RBC and a bachelor of arts in elementary education or a bachelor of music in K-12 music education from Cornerstone.

RBC also hosted a program with Trinity Evangelical Divinity School of Deerfield, Illinois. Trinity offered graduate-level classes on RBC's campus beginning in 1994. After a few years, the college ended that arrangement and did more to establish cooperative agreements with colleges in the Grand Rapids area.

Expanded educational opportunities have been a focus of the school from the very beginning. In its early existence, RBI offered courses in first aid, nursing, and secretarial skills. Today, the collaboration between Kuyper College and Cornerstone University is made available to students studying a variety of majors including accounting, marketing, exercise science, psychology, environmental biology, audio production, journalism, and more.

The second-floor atrium has always been a popular gathering place.

## North Central Association Accreditation

Besides the new location and new campus, other changes were taking place. In 1991, the school decided to pursue accreditation with the North Central Association (part of the Higher Learning Commission) while continuing accreditation with the Accrediting Association of Bible Colleges (AABC). RBC had been accredited by the AABC since 1964, and in 1970, the school became authorized by the State of Michigan Department of Education to grant

The student body, faculty, and staff gather for a photo in the Boonstra Fitness Center.

The main entrance of the college (pictured here in 1991) is on the third floor of the academic building and provides access to the business and academic offices, library, and classrooms. A reception desk has since been added.

The residents of the third floor of Timmer Hall are pictured here in 1992. The Timmer Hall dormitory is named for the school's first instructor, Johanna Timmer.

Since the 1940s, students have taken the initiative to publish a yearbook that for many years was called *The Echo*. The 1993 yearbook staff is pictured here in the atrium of the DeWitt Student Center.

bachelor of religious education degrees. The school received accreditation with the North Central Association on April 26, 1995, after a long period of self-study and reporting.

Though the new accreditation meant broader visibility for the school, the focus remained the same. RBC continued to teach Bible college curriculum and required students to major in Bible and theology. But the new accreditation was a significant step forward for the school in a number of ways. First, students would find it much easier to transfer credits to and from RBC to other colleges and universities in the United States and Canada. Second, some foundations that give grants to educational institutions required this level of accreditation before a grant is given. Finally, corporations who matched employee donations often required regional accreditation before giving matching funds.

Dr. Paul Bremer, then the vice president for academic administration, emphasized this focus. "We intend to continue as a Bible college that prepares students for work in church and missions. But now RBC will receive wider recognition for the education it provides," he stated. As a college accredited by the North Central Association, RBC grew in stature among other colleges in the area and of its type while retaining its initial purpose to train students to spread the gospel.

## Dr. Nicholas V. Kroeze Appointed President

Upon the announcement of the retirement of Dr. Edwin D. Roels in 1995, the school began its search for the fourth president. After reviewing a wide range of applicants, the search committee recommended Dr. Nicholas V. Kroeze to the board.

Dr. Nicholas V. Kroeze became the fourth president of the Reformed Bible College in 1995 after Dr. Edwin D. Roels retired.

Dr. Roger Greenway led the search committee as chairman. "The decision to nominate Dr. Kroeze was reached after a great deal of prayer and deliberation. From the first meeting on, the committee determined to bathe the search process in prayer and it did so," he said. "We were looking for a man of God who had a contagious faith and a missionary vision. And we believe that we have found such a man."

Dr. Kroeze had previously served as vice president for student affairs at Dordt College in Iowa and assistant principal at Kalamazoo Christian High School in Michigan. He

Students pose for a picture in 1991 on the sign at the front entrance to the new campus on the East Beltline.

This 1991 photo of the new Zondervan Library shows the card catalogs that were used before the library collection records were available to patrons on computer databases.

Students often study near the entrance to the Zondervan Library on the second floor. The waterfall on the first floor of the atrium was created by President Nick Kroeze and features the text of Revelation 22:1–2.

and his wife Gloria had also served as missionaries to Mexico for seven years.

Upon his appointment, President Kroeze addressed the RBC community. "There are today three stones of remembrance—hallmarks for our actions. First, we are to be people of prayer. Second, we are to make a commitment to Christian living. And third, we are to be a serving community."

President Kroeze, who is still currently serving as president, ushered the school into the digital era and guided the school through major changes, including a name change from Reformed Bible College to Kuyper College. Dr. Kroeze, who is a skilled woodworker, has donated several pieces of artwork to the school, including a twenty-foot tall waterfall titled "The River" that he inscribed with the words from Revelation 22:1-2 and a communion table for the chapel. Dr. Kroeze also implemented the tradition of presenting graduates with a lamp at commencement, a symbol and reminder to go forth and be a "light to the world."

*Chapter 8*

# Enriching Lives through Program and Enrollment Growth: 1995–2006

From 1995 to 2006, the college continued to grow and develop, adapting to many new changes in technology and higher education. The school had appointed Dr. Nicholas V. Kroeze as president in 1995, had received widely recognized accreditation from the North Central Association, and was beginning to incorporate digital technology into everyday use. But at the core, the mission of Reformed Bible College remained the same.

"I am eager to affirm that RBC highly values and remains dedicated to its calling of locating, encouraging, training, and sending people into full-time kingdom ministry," wrote President Kroeze in 1999. "We sense a very clear purpose and desire in serving the church as a unique institution of higher learning. We are privileged to have as our calling and focus such direct involvement in global witness. We are privileged too to have a broad and diverse family of supporters that enable people responding to God's call to concentrate more on training and less on financing."

RBC's tuition remained the lowest compared to eight other Christian colleges in the United States with Reformed roots with a yearly cost of $6,450 in 1995. Enrollment remained steady between 150 and 200. About 40 percent of RBC's operating budget was covered by tuition, and the difference was met with donations from individuals and churches and fees from campus rentals.

## Academic Program Developments

In 1996, RBC appointed Fred Sterenberg as the first director of the new EXCEL degree-completion program. The program was designed for adult learners who had an average of two years worth of college credit but who hadn't finished their education. Students could enroll in EXCEL and take courses during the evening, one night a week, for four hours at a time and were also expected to spend about fifteen hours per week studying on their own.

In 1971, the school was named Reformed Bible College (RBC) until it was renamed Kuyper College in 2006.

On nice days, students can be found studying outdoors on the lawn near the dorms or between the academic building and student center.

degrees to graduates. Since 1971, the college had offered bachelor of religious education degrees to students, but with expanded offerings and a higher level of academic accreditation from the North Central Association, a more universally recognized degree was desirable. In addition, students would be eligible to receive state financial aid under the new degree. The first bachelor of science degrees were given to fourteen graduates in 1998 and the degree has been used ever since.

## New Traditions Celebrate Foundational Values

At commencement in 1996, President Kroeze started a new tradition: presenting graduates with a lamp or candleholder. The lamps symbolized the college's challenge to its graduates: "go, and let your light shine."

President Kroeze designed the current version of the lamps, which contain seven different types of wood. Each wood represents a different area of the world and is symbolic of the college's emphasis on missions and diversity—around the world and within the student body. Hard Maple, Canarywood, Red Oak, Honduras Mahogany, English Walnut, Mexican Rosewood, and African Ebony are used in each lamp.

In addition to the lamp tradition, at the suggestion of the board, the school established the H. J. Kuiper Founder's Service Award in

After only three years, however, the college discontinued EXCEL because the program was not generating enough income to support itself. Despite the lack of a continuing program dedicated to degree completion, many non-traditional students have studied part-time at RBC to finish their degree since then.

In 1997, Reformed Bible College received approval to begin offering bachelor of science

In 1996, RBC launched EXCEL, a degree-completion program for adult learners. The program was active until 1998.

President Nick Kroeze developed the tradition of giving graduates a lamp upon graduation as a reminder for students to "go, and let your light shine." The tradition began in 1996.

The current design of the lamp given to graduates of the college features seven different types of wood from around the world.

DO THIS IN REMEMBRANCE OF ME

FROM EVERY TRIBE AND LANGUAGE AND PEOPLE AND NATION

President Nick Kroeze is an accomplished woodworker and has completed several projects for the school. This communion table was dedicated in 2000 and contains seven different types of wood from around the world representing the diversity of God's kingdom and the global focus of the college.

recognition of one of the school's founders and the first chairman of the board. The award was created to recognize individuals whose lifelong service to God exemplified the purpose and spirit of RBC.

Each year, the award is handed out at the Spring Gala. The award itself is the same as the lamps awarded to students upon graduation as a symbol of the light of Christ they bring to a needy world. They symbolize the global outreach of the college and the diverse ingathering of students who attend.

The first recipients of the award in 1997 were Marguerite Bonnema (1942), Mary De Boer VandenBosch (1942), and Andrew VanderVeer, the founders of Bethany Christian Services. Every year since

Reformed Bible College became debt free in 1997, despite the $11 million cost of the new campus completed only seven years earlier. President Nick Kroeze and board member and campus developer Dan Vos had the honor of burning the mortgage in a ceremony in the Boonstra Fitness Center.

then, God's faithfulness has been joyfully celebrated by recognizing the kingdom work of each award recipient.

## Reformed Bible College Becomes Debt Free

The move to and construction of the new campus was a costly endeavor, but by God's grace, the college was able to become debt free in 1997. The overall costs for the initial building phase of the library, dormitory, apartment building, classroom building, and existing building renovations for the student center, and for the later building phase that included the Boonstra Fitness Center, totaled $11 million.

Some large donations from several major donors (including the gift of the chapel) and many other smaller donations from over 2,500 contributors helped defray the cost, and payments from the sale of the old campus to Aquinas College were still being collected. A "mortgage burning" ceremony was held on campus on February 27, 1997, to mark the occasion.

President Kroeze spoke at the event, saying, "Now that the campus is complete and the construction debt paid, we are most grateful to God. More of the donations to the college can now be used for student scholarships and for development of exciting new programs." God provided adequate financial resources throughout the school's history, and He continued to bless the endeavors of the school as it expanded.

## Further Campus Changes

From 1997 to 1998, after a period of twenty years where enrollment remained steady, Reformed Bible College was blessed with a 43 percent increase in the number of students. Students were packed into the

Josh and Mandy Shaarda met at RBC in 1997, married, graduated, and headed for Africa, following the Lord as He led them into the mission field in 2001.

Josh Shaarda (2000) and Mandy Beute (1999) grew up in Michigan—Josh in McBain and Mandy about one hundred miles to the south in Hudsonville. Josh came to Kuyper intent on becoming a pastor. "The greatest benefits I received at the College were in terms of life calling, direction and values." Mandy went to Kuyper with missions in mind. "I loved the beautiful campus, the size, and that it felt like a family. All of that plus the emphasis on missions, the personable staff and spiritual atmosphere—not to mention that it was very affordable—I knew this was where God wanted me to be. And it was everything I hoped it would be."

From 2001 to 2005 the Shaardas served in Mahula in the Democratic Republic of Congo. "By 2003 we had a number of people who wanted to be baptized," said Josh. "That year we saw 11 baptisms. By the time the Lord called us to Uganda, the church was strong and had 24 baptized believers."

Josh and Mandy, together with their four children, now serve in Soroti, Uganda, where a civil war has left 20,000 widows and 100,000 orphans within a fifty-mile radius of their house. In addition, AIDS has affected almost everyone in the region. In Soroti, the Shaardas train Christian leaders at Bethel Bible College and teach pastors in rural areas that have little formal education.

Students frequently lead worship in chapel, which is held on Monday, Wednesday, and Friday each week. This picture shows the chapel worship band in 1998.

The Timmer Hall dormitory, pictured here in winter 1997, was the only suite-style dormitory until Schaal Hall was built in 1999.

To address the growing need for more dormitory space, RBC completed a new dormitory, Schaal Hall, in 1999 at a cost of $1,694,272. The new dormitory had capacity for sixty-four students and a resident director.

one existing dormitory building and one apartment building where three students often lived in a typically two-student dorm room. More students meant more space was desperately needed, so plans were made for another dormitory building.

The new dormitory was completed in the summer of 1999 and could house sixty-four students, along with a resident director. The total cost for the building, including furniture and equipment, came to $1,694,272. A dedication ceremony for the new building was held on October 16, 1999, and was named Schaal Residence Hall after board and faculty member Rev. John H. Schaal, who spoke at the ceremony. The existing residence hall was then formally named Timmer Residence Hall after college founder and faculty member Johanna Timmer.

While the new dormitory was being built, a maintenance building was also constructed through a generous gift from Dan R. Vos.

## Majors and Course Offering Expansion

Once the school received permission to offer a bachelor of science degree to graduates, new and existing course offerings and academic majors were developed and expanded. The school soon received permission to grant a bachelor of social work (BSW). The school had been offering courses in social work since the 1970s, but the new degree would allow students to receive a higher level of education. When the Council on Social Work Education accredited the program in 2006, RBC was only the second Bible college in the nation to offer an accredited BSW degree.

Another landmark course offering for the school occurred with the implementation of a TESOL (Teaching English to Speakers of Other Languages) class in 2001. The single course would later be expanded into a certificate program.

Several notable faculty members joined the school during this era:

- Dr. Dan Kroeze was hired to teach biblical studies in 1999.

Members of the 2000 RBC soccer club stretch before a game. The maintenance building in the background was built in 1999 through a generous gift from Dan R. Vos.

Students lounge on the soccer field in 2001.

- Dr. Doug Felch was appointed to RBC in 1999 as a theology professor.
- Greg Scott became the school's first full-time social work professor in 1999.
- Dr. Gary Teja was appointed in 2000 as a cross-cultural studies professor.
- In 2000, Dr. Melvin Flikkema was appointed as provost of the college.

He had served as the director of field education at the school since 1993.
- Dr. Judi Ravenhorst-Meerman, a 1991 graduate of RBC, was also hired as a social work professor in 2001.
- Rev. Evan Heerema was hired as the school's director of field education in 2001.

A student studies in the Zondervan Library in 2005.

Students enjoy a recreational room near the dining hall in the DeWitt Student Center. In 2008 this room was divided and remodeled into two weight and cardio fitness rooms.

- Teresa Renkema was hired in 2002 as a professor of intercultural communication and the director of the TESOL program.
- Rev. Brian Telzerow was appointed in 2003 as a youth ministry professor.
- Dr. Carol Hochhalter was hired in 2004 as a worship professor.
- Dr. Lisa Garvelink was hired in 2005 as an English professor.

## The Zondervan Library

The Reformed Bible College's Zondervan Library has been a hub for students and faculty members since it was formed early in the college's existence. Through generous donations from many, including a large donation from the family of H. J. Kuiper, and through the excellent care of several dedicated employees, the library quickly became the academic center of Reformed Bible College.

Since 1987, the library has been under the direction of Dianne Zandbergen. Michelle Norquist, the library's second professional librarian, was hired in 1994. The library also hires five to eight part-time student workers who assist patrons and perform a variety of other essential tasks.

Dr. Burt Braunius teaches a class on Christian education.

The Reformed Bible College choir has been performing since the early days of the institute.

# "Fifty-Two Flags" *by Dr. Nicholas V. Kroeze, President*

*This article originally appeared in the Spring 1996 RBC Newsletter. Today, there are fifty-seven flags hanging in the Boonstra Fitness Center gym representing countries where Kuyper alumni are currently serving.*

There are fifty-two flags hanging from the ceiling of the Boonstra Fitness Center on the campus of RBC. The fifty-two flags are not banners celebrating victories in sports. Neither are they symbols of political alignments nor attempts at bettering international public relations. These flags are symbolic of the locations RBC alumni have gone in response to the call the Lord has placed in their hearts to be of witness to Him. These flags do two other things: they are our own reminder of the "cloud of witnesses" which testify to the faithful response of His children, and they are also a constant reminder to pray for those who have given themselves to full-time kingdom service.

The stories and information you read in this newsletter focus on the "outcomes" of our alumni activities. You will clearly and easily note that "success" is measured in a way unique to a college which emphasizes ministry activity and impact. The tool used to measure success is "outcomes" or, rather, as we prefer to see it, as the "fruit of your labor." So, you will see two levels of fruit being born from the activity of Reformed Bible College: that following the labor of faculty and staff to educate, train, and inspire our graduates and that coming from the graduates themselves as they enter their fields of ministry.

As we look at those flags in the fitness center and are reminded of fruit that is born from faithful service, we are inspired and encouraged in the role this college has in God's kingdom-building work. We are blessed to see how He has touched the hearts and lives of many people in and through Reformed Bible College. We are blessed to work with students who desire to put His kingdom first. We are blessed to have professors and staff whose spiritual insight prepare us all for higher levels of service. We are blessed to receive the generous gifts of many donors. We are blessed to benefit from board members and others who volunteer their time and energy. We thank our Lord for these blessings and pray that we may continue faithfully in the calling He has given us. Thank you for your part in bringing His Word to our needy world!

The library's mission continues to be the provision of facilities, resources, and services that support the curriculum of the college. Library patrons can search the online catalog and electronic databases at one of a number of computer stations. One computer station desk was custom built by President Kroeze. As the library moves towards a "learning commons" model of service, students now have access to the services provided by the academic support staff and the writing center tutors, all within the library itself.

The Zondervan Library is a member of the Cornerstone University Library Network (CULN), a collaborative network of Cornerstone's and Grand Rapids Theological Seminary's Miller Library, the Puritan Reformed Theological Seminary Library, and Kuyper College's (RBC changed its name in 2006) Zondervan Library. Together this network of libraries provides access to over 200,000 resources. The Zondervan Library is a member of a number of other library consortiums and as a result has interlibrary loan privileges with libraries across the United States.

Today, the library's collection consists of approximately 72,000 print volumes and 80,000 electronic volumes. The library provides access to thousands of full-text journal articles and also includes the Zondervan Collection, a special collection of approximately 4,000 volumes. The Zondervan® Publishers graciously contributes one copy of each book and Bible they publish to the college.

Dr. Burt Braunius and his wife donated this Computer Ministry Center in the library in 1997.

Dianne Zandbergen and Michelle Norquist are the Zondervan Library's two full-time librarians and are pictured here in 1998.

The two-story Zondervan Library is located near the campus entrance and is accessible from within the academic building.

*Chapter 9*

# Same Heart, Same Spirit, Same Mission: 2006–2014

In 2006, Reformed Bible College faced new changes and new challenges. How would the school continue to be relevant in a changing world? The answer was a repositioning strategy that would meld the mission of the school from its beginning with preparing students for the ever-evolving needs of today's culture.

One of the changes made during the repositioning was the college's tagline. More than a "slogan," the tagline became a purpose statement reflecting the college's mission-minded focus: "Bringing God's Grace into Today's Culture." The emphasis noted in the statement is what founders envisioned in 1939: a straightforward, practical application of God's Word.

Two thousand six was a year of introspection and self-examination for the college. Nineteen majors were available to students at the college and 51 percent of students were enrolled in the three most popular programs: social work, youth ministry, and pre-seminary. Enrollment was up 21 percent over the previous year, and the student body was comprised of 23 percent multicultural students. And students continued to be a blessing in the community surrounding them: 79 percent of the college's seniors were involved in classroom-driven service learning.

Over the last seventy-five years of the college's existence, one thing that has changed dramatically is technology. The majority of students now own a laptop and a smartphone, and once-popular study locations like public computer stations and computer labs are being used more and more infrequently as personal computing is on the rise. Online classes and assignments have become common. Students are now being regularly challenged to "bring God's grace into today's culture" in places like the Internet. The world's online expansion offers unique challenges and opportunities for the college, as online tools like websites, blogs, and social media networks are connecting people in new and different ways.

Kuyper College course and program offerings have also expanded significantly in the last decade. A sports ministry major, an English professional studies major, and a business major were added, among others. By 2012, Kuyper College offered thirty-one majors, fourteen minors, and a variety of concentrations or emphases and certificate programs.

Kuyper College's student body includes a number of international students. Kuyper alumni include graduates from countries like Brazil, Canada, Germany, Great Britain, Guatemala, Japan, Korea, Mongolia, the Netherlands, Nepal, Sierra Leone, Thailand, and Zambia.

# Abraham Kuyper *by Carlos Hidalgo*

"There is not a square inch in the whole domain of our human existence over which Christ, who is Sovereign over all, does not cry: 'Mine!'"—Abraham Kuyper.

Abraham Kuyper, an extraordinary and historic figure, was a pastor, theologian, scholar, journalist, educator, and statesman. Though beginning in the parish ministry, he moved on to become editor of two Christian periodicals, founded the first Dutch political party and the first Christian Democratic party in the world, and established the Free University in Amsterdam (a Christian university founded on Reformed worldview principles). He served as prime minister of the Netherlands from 1901 to 1905. He was also a courageous advocate for equality regardless of social status, race, or gender at a time when that notion was not the overwhelming sentiment of the day.

Kuyper articulated more clearly than anyone the importance of recognizing that everyone has a worldview—a personal and also corporate way of perceiving and interacting with reality. Kuyper taught us that we must discover and understand what this means to each individual and to the mind and systems of the culture we are trying to reach with God's word and grace. This is the essence of effectively carrying out God's great commission throughout the world.

As Kuyper explained it, a worldview that is Reformed in character holds that all of life is to be lived unto the glory of God. In this, there is no area of life not subject to the Lordship of Christ, the witness of the believer, and the work of the church. The Bible is the inspiration, insight, and guide that informs, instructs, and motivates the Christian to give effective witness in the context of his and her day. The direct application of scriptures into every area of our lives, and in addressing the nature of the world around us, makes our faith both a public as well as private matter.

Today, Kuyperian cultural and social thought, along with his biblical worldview, are the subject of theological, scholarly, and societal studies at the Kuyper Center for Public Theology at Princeton Theological Seminary, the Kuyper Scholars Program at Dordt College, the Kuyper Foundation in England, and at seminars in colleges and seminaries throughout the world.

## Changing the Name to Kuyper College

In 2001, the board of RBC began discussing a possible name change for the college. President Kroeze noted the most important thing surrounding the discussion was the school's ultimate identity. "What we are known by is not as important as what we are known for. Our identity, ultimately, is not this beautiful campus nor the name we cherish. Our identity is the God who gave us the calling to prepare men and women for lives of kingdom-focused service," he wrote in the November 2001 *Reformed Bible College News Magazine*.

The board voted in April 2002 to move forward in the process of changing the school's name. One name strongly considered was Ambassador College but another organization had used the name so the idea was discarded. Other names discussed were Anchor College, Beacon College, Providence College, and Wellspring College, but the issue was tabled in April 2003.

But soon after the issue was set aside, the board resumed the discussion again in October 2004. On October 20, 2005, the board decided to begin the process to change the school's name to Kuyper College, after the Dutch theologian and statesman Abraham Kuyper. The name change was implemented in 2006 after much prayer and discussion.

Two years after the name change, President Kroeze reflected, "This effort has been terrifically hard but incredibly beneficial. It has demanded that the College analyze itself, study the market, meet higher accreditation standards, clarify its sense of identity and fit, and attract more students and resources. These have been healthy, appropriate and necessary demands

The school was called Reformed Bible College from 1971 until the name was changed to Kuyper College in 2006.

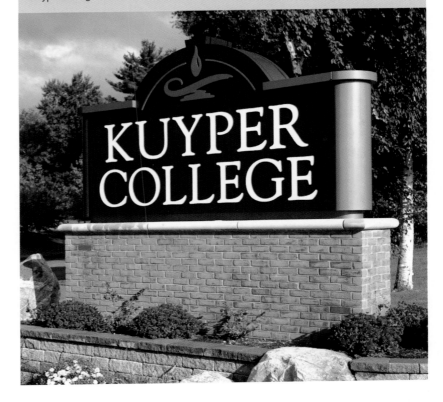

Dr. Dan Kroeze teaches a Bible class in 2010.

for the College to respond to. The process has energized the institution and has given board members, faculty and staff a refreshed sense of personal and professional motivation that are contributing to the welfare and success of this institution."

Enrollment also increased as a result of the name change. New student enrollment increased 21 percent in 2006–2007, and 39 percent over that figure in 2007–2008. In 2012, a record seventy-four students graduated from the school and enrollment and graduation numbers continue to remain strong.

Dr. Lisa Garvelink teaches a literature class in 2009.

Dr. Branson Parler, associate professor of theological studies, teaches a class in 2010.

Music and worship major students study in the music lab, located in the library, with Dr. Carol Hochhalter in 2006.

The first year Kuyper College participated in the National Christian College Athletic Association with men and women's basketball was in 2007. The 2007–2008 men's basketball team ended their inaugural season with a 16-13 record.

Casey the Cougar was chosen as the school mascot by student vote and is pictured here in the student section at a 2007 basketball game. Casey is the phonetic spelling of "K. C.," the abbreviation of Kuyper College.

## Kuyper College Adds an Athletic Program

In April 2006, after eighteen months of studying the idea and years of discussion, the Kuyper College Board of Trustees overwhelmingly approved a recommendation from the college's athletic taskforce to establish an athletic program—the first organized sports at the school in decades. "The athletic program will have a focus that parallels our mission," said President Kroeze. "We want the spiritual development of athletes to be as important as competition." With that in mind, Kuyper applied for membership in the National Christian College Athletic Association (NCCAA), an

organization dedicated to helping its member schools equip student-athletes and coaches with the necessary tools to make a positive and meaningful impact for Christ.

One main component built into the athletic program was an emphasis on outreach. Through the athletic program, Kuyper's outreach would be extended to opposing teams (both Christian and non-Christian) and the community through sportsmanship, relationship building, prayer and devotions, and mission trips.

The athletic program began in the fall of 2007 with both men's and women's basketball teams. Casey the Cougar was chosen by student vote to be a mascot. The first basketball game was held on October 20

The inaugural women's basketball team in 2007–2008 ended the season with a 9-13 record.

in the Boonstra Fitness Center against opponent Grace Bible College of Grand Rapids. The women's team, though they scored the first official points of a Kuyper College sports team, lost after a tough battle, but the men's team got their first victory and the first ever win for an official Kuyper College sports team. The women's team ended the inaugural season with a 9-13 record and the men's team ended the season with a 16-13 record.

In 2010, Kuyper College added women's volleyball and men's soccer teams, both of which had previously been club sports. In the fall of 2013, men's and women's cross country teams were added to the school's athletic program.

In 2010, women's volleyball (pictured above) and men's soccer were added to the college's athletic program.

## Academic Partnerships with Other Institutions

In addition to the collaboration created with Cornerstone University in 1994, Kuyper College has continued to pursue relationships with other local institutions. Collaboration with Calvin College and Grand Rapids Community College provided Kuyper students with expanded course options. A unique collaborative agreement with Davenport University allowed students to earn two degrees—one from each institution—in just five years.

Dr. Judi Ravenhorst-Meerman teaches social work students in 2010. The Council of Social Work Education accredits the social work program.

Every year the college hosts a gala to celebrate God's faithfulness to Kuyper College. Recent galas, like this one pictured in 2012, have been held at Frederick Meijer Gardens.

Kuyper College graduates are also given advanced standing at several post-graduate institutions. An accelerated pre-seminary program was developed with Calvin Theological Seminary and Grand Rapids Theological Seminary. Kuyper pre-seminary students can transfer to either school following their third year at Kuyper College, with three seminary courses transferring back to Kuyper for completion of the bachelor of science degree. This allows students to graduate from Kuyper College at the end of their fourth year and graduate from seminary with a master of divinity (MDiv) two years later, reducing the combined length of the two programs from seven years down to six years. Discussions have begun with Western Theological Seminary to establish a similar program with Kuyper College. Furthermore, the social work program has been recognized as one of the top programs in the state so graduates receive advanced standing at many graduate schools.

These collaborative programs are a far cry from the Reformed Bible Institute's early years. RBI did not receive accreditation until the 1950s and few classes before then counted at the college level. RBI students who wished to further their education often had to retake undergraduate courses before applying to seminary or postgraduate institutions. Today, Kuyper College graduates are held in high regard and are highly sought after in many fields.

## The MERGE Experience

During the 2011–2012 school year, the college established the MERGE Experience, a unique, first-of-its-kind program designed to help incoming students enter into the world of college life and academic responsibilities. MERGE focuses on five components: Worldview, Identity Development,

The orientation staff made up of faculty, staff, and upperclassmen welcomed freshman and new students to campus in 2007. Orientation for new students is now part of the MERGE Experience.

As part of the MERGE Experience, new students participate in team-building games like this one at Camp Roger during orientation in 2013.

Intercultural Competency, Engaged Learning, and Leadership—components the college has emphasized since it began. The MERGE Seminar is a two-credit class taken in a student's first semester. MERGE Service Learning is a two-credit course taken second semester in which students act intentionally and thoughtfully in response to discoveries made in the MERGE Seminar, though each component is woven through every course.

As part of the worldview component, students are encouraged to formulate and articulate a biblical worldview and learn how to interact with people who may have conflicting worldviews. Students in MERGE are also encouraged to develop a healthy identity by engaging in experiential learning, case studies, and other active learning strategies.

Students can be found working on-campus jobs in the cafeteria, library, writing center, front desk, maintenance, and more.

Named after William and Martha DeWitt, the student center was created by remodeling the existing Sunshine Community Church building in 1989. The cafeteria, fitness rooms, student mailboxes, and Student Life offices are located in this building.

Furthermore, the MERGE Experience challenges students to develop awareness of one's own culture, attitude toward cultural differences, cultural knowledge and understanding, and cross-cultural skills and behaviors. Students are also encouraged to engage in an active and disciplined learning process by developing the foundation of good critical thinking—knowing oneself—so they can use their growing skills through the knowledge of their strengths and weaknesses to analyze, evaluate, and discern meaning and truth from every learning experience as a guide to belief and action.

Finally, Kuyper College teaches a relational model of leadership that is inclusive, empowering, purposeful, ethical, and process oriented. MERGE helps students understand that leadership is taking responsibility for where God has placed them with the skill set He has given them and being faithful to God's call on their lives. Although there is not one identifiable right way to lead a group, Kuyper teaches that leadership is a process of cultivating one's worldview, understanding self (identity), learning how to connect with others, and engaging God's world.

## Student Life

Since the beginning of the Reformed Bible Institute in 1939 to its seventy-fifth anniversary in 2014, much has changed. The fact that many meaningful, lifelong relationships begin because of friendships forged at the college remains constant. Those relationships begin in the dormitories, in the classroom, and around campus through official and unofficial student activities organized by the college and students themselves.

Today, students enjoy a variety of school-sponsored activities throughout the school

# Alumni Spotlight:
# Lloyd Ng'ambi, Class of 2010

Born in a small African village in the high mountains of Zambia's Northern Province, Lloyd Ng'ambi struggled to survive the early years of his life. By the time he was five, his mother and his siblings had died and he often went hungry, sometimes managing to eat only one meal a day. He would walk barefoot to school, a three-hour journey each way, and spent every spare moment doing manual labor for neighbors so he could pay the school fees.

By the age of nineteen, Ng'ambi finished primary school and received a scholarship to a secondary school. While he was there, he found friends that introduced him to Christ. "I accepted Jesus Christ as my personal savior, and dedicated my life to serving Him from then on," said Ng'ambi. He eventually went to Zomba Theological Seminary and became a part-time youth pastor.

Because of a pastor's encouragement, Ng'ambi enrolled at Kuyper College and received a bachelor's degree in youth ministry in 2010. While he studied in the United States, his wife Annah and their three children remained in Zambia. He only saw them once during that entire time, during a return trip to Zambia provided by funds raised by students, faculty, and staff.

Ng'ambi is now the parish minister of Chilenje Church in a suburb of Lusaka. He is also the full-time synod youth coordinator for the CCAP in Zambia, training youth leaders and developing youth programs to address the challenges facing the youth of Zambia. "Young people don't just want to be seen in the church; they want to be welcomed as contributing members," he said. "I want to develop youth programs in Zambia that address the needs of our young people holistically, spiritually, physically and emotionally, equipping them with the Word of God."

Each residence hall floor has a student resident assistant (RA) that leads weekly floor Bible studies.

Over the years, Timmer Hall and Schaal Hall have had both male and female floors, but in recent years Timmer Hall has been a men's dormitory and Schaal Hall has been a women's dorm.

year. Orientation begins with various social events like volunteering in the community, small student groups, and campus-wide events like Fun Fest or the O-Show, a funny look at traditions and life on campus presented to freshman by upperclassmen. Other events through the year include Taste of Grand Rapids and Taste of the World events, the annual Christmas banquet, a variety show, choir tours, and much more.

Other student activities are more serious in nature and seek to solve a problem or bring awareness to particular issues. The student-run HANDS (Helping And Nurturing During Service) Committee hosts speakers and events to teach students and community members about social issues in the community and around the world. Students also frequently lead chapel services, Bible studies, and worship sessions for their peers.

In 2012, the college held its first annual Student Scholar Day and Faculty Scholar Day as a celebration of academic scholarship. The now-annual event features the work of many talented students and faculty members who present on a wide variety of scholarly work.

Chapel is held every Monday, Wednesday, and Friday and is well attended by students, faculty, and staff.

Students can also take advantage of the opportunity to work on campus to help offset the cost of tuition. Student employment opportunities are available at the front desk, library, cafeteria, and elsewhere. Employment on campus not only allows students to earn some extra money, but it also provides students with professional experience that will be useful in later careers.

Students of the college from its beginning through today have expressed how much they appreciated the tone of student life on campus. Alumni of the college frequently look back fondly on their days at the school recalling friends, dormitory life, and communal worship and study. Above all, the work and ministry of Kuyper College is about relationships with others and together serving the God of the Universe.

Graduation ceremonies are held across the street from campus in the Sunshine Community Church building.

The end of the academic school year is celebrated each spring with an all-school picnic on the lawn by the chapel.

A new gold-clad cross was installed on the chapel in 2013 to honor Dan Vos, who passed away in 2012, and to celebrate the college's seventy-fifth anniversary. The cross on the chapel is the highest point on campus.

*Chapter 10*

# "To the Only Wise God"
## by President Nicholas V. Kroeze

"To the only wise God be glory forever through Jesus Christ! Amen." These are the words Paul chose to conclude his letter to the Romans as recorded in Chapter 16, verse 27. Paul undoubtedly pondered all he had written to the Romans—general theology, human history, instruction for living—and stepped back amazed at how all these things come together so fully, so completely, so wonderfully under God's knowledge, love, and grace. God, knowing the truth about everything, determines the best course of action in order to obtain the best result. And He achieves it. Such is God's wisdom!

We who have a connection with Kuyper College likewise stand back amazed. Even over a "brief" seventy-five years and as a small institution in the grander fellowship of colleges and universities, we have enough—more than enough—that gives testimony "to the only wise God" and His blessing upon the mission that drew our founders together and which still compels—and propels—us into the future. Indeed, if we were to say we have had success at anything, it is the extent to which we have witnessed God's hand in our history and the glory rendered to His name through our alumni, employees, trustees, and supporters whose primary goal has been to serve Christ's church and His world.

When I think about Paul's conclusion in connection with our future and what to convey in this final chapter of the book, I am not so much drawn to plans and programs as I am to the spirit and character of Kuyper College. Time and time again I have heard from any number and variety of people "there's something really unique about Kuyper." Those of you with some connection to the college know well of what I'm referring to. For visitors who have only stepped into this environment for a brief moment, they sense it almost immediately and come away acknowledging, "Yes, there's something there" they seem to have "mysteriously" sensed.

I believe, in line with Paul, it comes down to a keen awareness that it is God who is working in and through every aspect of the college—accomplishing His wise will—and we are part of a historical and eternal story of heavenly proportions. Yes, we want to educate students well. Yes, we want to be professional in our administration of the college. Yes, we want to provide a solid financial base. Yes, we want to attract more students. "Yes" to all of these and more things that would characterize us as "successful." But there is something *so much more* pervading the daily activities and long-range plans of the college: I have to say it is, quite simply, the *joy of the Lord* that we hold in our hearts and celebrate together. This college is about and for *Him*. We are about seeking *His* wisdom. Our celebrations are about *His* glory. These thoughts are what frame our vision of the future.

## The Mission of Kuyper College

Kuyper College equips students with a biblical, Reformed worldview to serve effectively Christ's church and His world.

## What Will Kuyper Look Like in Ten Years?

First and foremost, the *mission* of Kuyper College will be seen as even more vital and motivational in our sense of identity. Today, we are highly encouraged to see the global Christian community espousing the clarity of understanding and guidance to action as expressed through a biblical, Reformed worldview—particularly as articulated by Abraham Kuyper. The church is yearning to understand what it means to be Christian at a time when society is redefining itself, new social mores are being established, the relevance of and respect toward Christianity are challenged, and, yet, where the cry for social justice, humanitarian aid, spiritual peace, and a *Savior* grow ever-stronger.

Increasingly, Protestant *and Catholic* entities are discovering in Abraham Kuyper's thoughts a framework that helps the universal church be even more pertinent in the world over the coming decades. These are exciting times! Kuyper College

Student Fernando Anleu reviews classwork in the hallway by the Vos Chapel.

Student Dylan Kern studies in the Zondervan Library.

Current students Nicolas Van Veen, CJ Bussey, and Vanessa Rodriguez fellowship on a picnic table near the dormitories.

Laurel (Ritzema) Dykema (2010) participated in a May term class in Guatemala in 2008.

Lexie Oosse (2011) worked in Uganda to complete the requirements for her social work internship.

# Implications of Changing the Name to "Kuyper" College

When the board of the Reformed Bible College was discussing a possible name change for the school in 2005, Chairman Lloyd Vanderkwaak noted two decisions needed to be made. "One, we need to pick a name, and two, we need to ask the question, can we live up to that name? [The name] Kuyper does come with a standard that people already know: we are considering Kuyper because he had the ability to bring the scripture to the common man. We need to decide if the name goes with our vision and mission and if there are internal adjustments that need to be made."

Professor Teresa Renkema is the director of the TESOL program (Teaching English to Speakers of Other Languages).

Becky (Lockwood) De Dock (2011), center, worked in Uganda for her social work internship.

will strive to promote its mission and expand our ability to be a resource to the church through our ability to articulate well what it means to "bring God's grace into today's culture."

*Collaboration* will characterize our partnerships and opportunities to contribute to the development of students, the church, and other institutions. We have had a good beginning in building these relationships over the past several years as the quality of our programs and preparedness of our students have gained even more respect and regard amongst our sister institutions and the organizations into which our graduates enter their life's vocations. Kuyper is positioned well to have increasing influence and impact in the bigger picture of the church and global community by partnering with or being a resource to all entities whose common value is the glory of God in the name of Jesus Christ. Thus, Kuyper will participate with more intentionality in trans-denominational efforts to bring the saving and healing ministry of Christ throughout the world.

Our embodiment and articulation of *Reformed worldview* will take on broader significance and greater expression through the efforts of the college. A guiding characteristic of the college over our history has been that of *praxis*—taking knowledge, theory, and theology into practical application to address contemporary needs. Kuyper has been strong with the second part of that definition through its history and has more recently increased a complementary emphasis on the first part of the definition. We will see the importance of these two increase together over the coming years. Scholarship and application are a "steel sharpening steel" pairing that are making the college a more energized institution with a very

## Social Work Collaboration in Liberia

In 2006, Kuyper College social work professor Dr. Judi Ravenhorst-Meerman traveled to Monrovia, Liberia, with colleagues from Calvin College to explore the potential of collaboration with Mother Patern College of Health Sciences. Since then, Kuyper and Calvin have begun working with Mother Patern to expand their two-year social work degree program into a full-fledged four-year baccalaureate degree program. Civil wars raged in Liberia from 1989 to 2003 and social workers are needed to repair the wounds left from that time and the issues plaguing the population today.

Kuyper and Calvin faculty work with faculty at Mother Patern to create a curriculum structure, identify potential internship sites for Mother Patern students, and form relationships with key government officials. The first cohort of around twenty BSW students enrolled at Mother Patern in the fall of 2008. Kuyper College professors continue to travel to Liberia periodically to develop the program and train leaders and at the same time are gaining valuable insight into social work around the world.

Students Katilyn Leasure, Janet Whytock, Geralyn Folz, and Valerie VantLand talk in a dorm room in Schaal Hall.

David Weber, Kelly Oosterbroek, Cory Hendrickson, and Mat Finlay have a conversation after class.

## Kuyper College Seal

· With its motto, *ora et labora*—pray and work—the Kuyper College Seal reflects the purpose of the college—to equip God's people for Christian ministries throughout the world. Central to learning at Kuyper is the Word of God, represented by the symbol of a light-giving lamp. Surrounding the lamp are traditional Christian symbols: the crown of faith, the anchor of hope, and the cloak of loving service. The seal colors symbolize the kingship of Christ (gold), the sacrifice of the atonement (scarlet), and the priesthood of Christ (purple).

optimistic view of our place in higher education and society in the coming years.

Another pairing that has been and will continue to be of great importance to us is found in our college seal: *ora et labora*—pray and work. There is so much that can be said about prayer and its place in the life of Kuyper College—it pervades every hour of the day! A ready impression made on me the first day I came to Kuyper (which actually was when I came on campus back in 1971 to participate in Dr. Van Halsema's Summer Training Session) was that "these people love to pray!" Prayer was not seen as the customary way to start a day, start a meeting, or start a new project. *Ora et labora* was never understood to mean "pray and *then* work." Prayer permeated and punctuated life and activity throughout the day: prayer was the "normal" on-going conversation with God that rode on the surface of people's lives as they worked projects through. We treasure this vitality in the college today and note if we maintain an on-going conversation with God as we work, the nature of our work and our interaction with others are much more grace-filled and God-glorifying.

Josef Disby, a current student, studies outside Timmer Hall.

Jeremy Van Woerden (2009, first row, second from left) served in Indonesia to fulfill the requirements for his youth ministry internship.

Megan Ritsema (2012) completed her student teaching/internship in Beijing, China, in 2012.

Students Hyeon Chan Kim, Ben Hoekman, and Kevin Riemersma play music in the chapel.

Students Karla Velis and Caleb Horton enjoy a meal together in the dining hall.

*Labora* is the Latin word for "work" and *avodah* is the Hebrew counterpart. Interestingly, avodah also has another meaning: "worship." In essence, what the Hebrew word translates is "what a servant brings to the master." This, of course, could not be more apropos in the context of Kuyper College. The spirit with which we engage our daily activities is characterized as "worshipful." This attitude is evident in the way we strive to serve each other, it is critically clear in the morale evidenced by faculty and staff who work successfully with only marginal resources available, and it is seen in the readiness of students and employees to enfold those who are lonely, hurt, or in need of hope. *Avodah* is also what motivates the college toward academic and professional excellence—we want to do our best as unto the Lord. Kuyper College will continue to treasure this fuller sense of work over the coming decades for it is very much in the DNA of the institution stretching back to our founding. The practical expression of our love for God and humankind is manifested through the work that we do—and we love it! Certainly, *ora et labora* will remain much more than a symbol on our seal in the future of the college.

The stated *Core Values* of the college are becoming more of a foreground rather than background set of ideals we are striving to integrate throughout the planning and work of the college. Though a good way to look at this (as with all of the areas noted above) is that all these can be considered *foundational* to the life and work of the college, we have to be somewhat careful in doing so. If we conceive these as the *base* from which we are heading off into future directions—like the purpose for which a launchpad serves a rocket—we may have a picture that is somewhat misdirective. The image I'd rather we think of with regard to our Core Values is that of *girders*. Girders permeate the whole structure, giving it shape and strength, connecting across every aspect and tying them together, and serving as the framework upon which everything else is held and fastened. The girders, based in the foundation, go up first and the rest follows. The girders are also the structure upon which future expansion is connected so the whole remains contemporary and pertinent. This is how we increasingly see our Core Values at work in the planning and execution of plans at the college.

The role of our Core Values in the future will also be more prominent as criteria with which to safeguard the biblical integrity of the college and strengthen our stand in the public

## Core Values of Kuyper College

- *Primacy of Scripture*
  We believe that the Bible is the Word of God and must guide our teaching, philosophy, lifestyle, and response to our ministry or vocational calling.

- *Biblical Worldview*
  We believe history is directed and controlled by God—Father, Son, and Holy Spirit—toward the accomplishment of God's purposes for all creation. Education at Kuyper College is conducted within the framework of a biblical worldview from which students can assimilate, synthesize, and respond to situations of life and learning.

- *Reformed Doctrine*
  We understand and apply our faith and worldview according to the teachings of the Bible as summarized in the Heidelberg Catechism, the Canons of Dort, the Belgic Confession, and the Westminster Standards.

- *Academic Excellence*
  We emphasize the importance of cultivating the mind as primary in providing quality, Christian higher education.

- *Holistic Development*
  We strive to form world-class citizens who are academically, spiritually, socially, and morally discerning, just, and merciful leaders in church and society.

- *Caring Community*
  We actively work toward a campus environment, denominationally and ethnically diverse in nature, where mentoring, mutual care, accountability, and encouragement are characteristic of students, faculty, and staff.

Professor Greg Scott is the social work program director.

Student Jesslyn Bolthouse studies in the atrium near the Zondervan Library.

Student Rita Baraka discusses a lecture with a classmate.

arena as we see society manifest increasingly anti-biblical attitudes and behaviors. The meaning of our Core Values and our commitment to them will need to be studied, discussed, understood, and integrated more fully throughout the institution and with our supporting constituency. In this, we can also be a resource and encouragement to others through our expression of the Core Values and Kuyper's ability to define well what "bringing God's grace into today's culture" means in any and every decade, locally and around the world. These are exciting times! Kuyper College can engage them well and we will!

## Looking at It All

As I reflect on the contents of this book I am struck with how much more it is than "a trip down memory lane." Yes, it has been fun to recall some wonderful personalities, see the historical pictures, and feel the nostalgia of the people, places, and events that surrounded the lives of so many of us connected with RBI, RBC, and Kuyper. More wonderful still, however, is to have seen our anniversary theme of "By God's grace, for His glory" move from page to page to page. The history we have is the story of God's hand of blessing, His tangible presence through times of opportunity and times of challenge. The story of Kuyper College truly, then, is not a history but a *testimony*. I think this spirit of testimony is what best answers the question so often asked, "What is so unique about Kuyper?"

This precious testimony has been borne by every soul that has come in contact with the college. We must never think of any of those people noted in this book as "prominent" in our minds for there are thousands in the mix of unheralded alumni, dedicated faculty, supportive staff, visionary trustees, generous donors, and prayer warriors who are every bit as much valued in the eyes of God and in the heart of the college for the selfless dedication, effective service, and modeling of Christ that have characterized their lives and service before the Lord. Praise God for them! If there were a second answer to the question, "What is so unique about Kuyper?" I'd say it's a deep sense of *call*.

I didn't intend to drive to this point but in meditating on what to say in this summary it seems like I was led to characterize the college in terms similar to the two most important things that Christ reminded us of—God and our

Current students Austin Kammeraad and David Garrett study in a dorm room in Timmer Hall.

neighbor: "Love the Lord your God with all your heart and with all your soul and with all your mind. This is the first and greatest commandment. And the second is like it: Love your neighbor as yourself" (Matthew 22:37–38). Yes, there is uniqueness in Kuyper. It is the uniqueness of an institution that is—quite tangibly—in love with God and with our neighbors here and around the world. The highest degree and the best way we can express that love is what enlivens us. We are delighted when our work is seen to glorify God and brings help, hope, and love into the lives of others. This is the history of Kuyper College and we are eager to recognize it as the future of the college as well. We are blessed—thanks be to God!—and we will be a blessing to many others for decades to come.

*Soli Deo Gloria. Ora et labora.*

Rachel Visser, a current student, studies on the lawn near the dormitories.

Students Joelle Garcia, Marissa Foster, Jordyn Rietveld, and Cassie Lampen enjoy a meal in the dining hall.

Students Krista Vermeer and Alli Shear worship in the Vos Chapel.

Current students Nicole DeWindt and Gabe Mitogo climb the stairs in the atrium on their way to class.

Current Kuyper student Yanelis Castillo studies in the Zondervan Library.

**KUYPER COLLEGE**

CELEBRATING

*Years* 75

1939 — 2014

*By God's Grace*
*For His Glory*

This page represents a sample of the college community during the seventy-fifth anniversary year. Groups represented include board, faculty, staff, and students.

# Appendix A

# Appendix B

Former RBI/RBC/Kuyper College Faculty and Staff

Walter De Jong
Harvey DeJager
Kim Desgranges
Marjorie DeYoung
R. Joe Dieleman ('76)
Rev. Fred Diemer
Jack Dieterie
Liz Doornbos
Glenda Droogsma
Julie Dunning
Lance Ebenstein
Mary (Magee) Eelkema
June Ellison
Ann Essenburg ('06)
Michael Ferris
Melissa Finkbeiner
Dr. Melvin Flikkema
Dorothy Silvis Folkersma
Barry Foster ('75)
Sarah Fredricks ('42)
James Fridsma
Joyce VanderLinden Fynaardt ('60)
Theresa Glass ('95)
Cisco Gonzalez
Michelle Greydanus
Walter Griffioen
Margaret Grift ('93)
Katie J. Gunnink ('44)
Ken Haveman
Rev. Evan Heerema ('88)
Rev. Jacob Heerema
Sandra Hegeman ('79)
Clare Hempel
Winifred Hempel
Dr. Richard A. Hertel
Phyllis Hertel
Jack Hoekstra
Bea Hovinga Holtrop
Sylvia Douma Holtrop ('72)
Thomas Holwerda
Roy Hopp
Rev. Paul Hostetter

Dorothy Hostetter
Patricia Howe
Ruth Huizenga
Allison Hutt
Shar Jacobsma
Charles Jansen
William Jansen
Sylvia Kallemeyn ('74)
Larissa Kamps
Carolyn Kennedy ('88)
Kate Klemp
Kimberly Kolbe
Dr. George Kroeze
Janice Kuipers
Reka La Grand
Julius Levering
Helen Linders ('59)
Markay Lyon
Eleanor Mannes Maas ('68)
Dr. Jessica Maddox ('98)
Dr. William Masselink
Amanda Mclittle
Bernice Meeuwsen
John Menninga
Ben Meyer
Pearl Vander Kooi Meyer
Keith Meyering ('76)
Nella Mierop
Bertha VandePol Miersma ('42)
Joy Milano
Dr. Timothy Monsma
Jill Monte
Luke Morgan ('10)
Wesley Morgan
Gayle (Heyboer) Morse ('80)
Peter Nagelkerke
Lavonne Nettleton
Nylene Pruis Nol
Hermina Nyhof ('73)
James O'Brien
Dr. Lubbertus Oostendorp
Michael Palmer

Stephen Pettis
Jenny Postema
Jana Postma
Doralee Powell ('94)
Amy Rau ('07)
Sung-Ae Reed
Dr. James Ritsema
Joanne Spalink Rodgers
Dr. Edwin D. Roels
Jeffrey Roloff
Dr. Tamara Rosier
Pat Kuiper Rubingh
Sheryl Witteveen Rupke
Rev. John H. Schaal
Penelope Kooyers Schering
Connie Scheurwater ('82)
Janet Scholma
Janice Schregardus
Mary Schultze
Dr. Tom Schwanda
Dr. William Shell
Andrea Smith
Dr. Addison Soltau
Jeff Stam ('76)
Evonne Steenwyk ('68)
Kari Sterk ('06)
Thomas B. Sterk ('08)
Jack W. Stoepker
Ryan Struck-Vanderhaak
Todd Sytsma
Patricia Talen
Beverly Tanis ('63)
Dr. Gary Teja ('69)
Marilyn Thompson
Patricia Tigchelaar
Johanna Timmer
Allison Backous Troy
Betty Van Artsen
Judy Schreur Van Dobschutz
Dr. Dick L. Van Halsema
Mrs. Thea B. Van Halsema
Jack W. Van Laar

Julie VanDerVeen Van Til
A. Dean Vanbruggen
Nancy Vande Guchte
Karen VandeBerg ('78)
Joyce Vanden Berg ('75)
Julie L. Vandenberg
Sharron Vandenberg
Nelle Vander Ark
Helena Vander Ark ('87)
Mark Vander Ark
Ruth VanderKlay
Krinn K. VanderSloot
Eric VanderWall ('10)
Nadia A. VanDyk ('98)
Pao Vang
Delores VanHeuvelen
Ken VanProoyen
Ruth VanProoyen
Rev. Rolf Veenstra
Bernard H. Velzen
Eugene Ver Hage
Gladys VerMeulen
William VerMeulen ('74)
Kenneth VerSteeg ('69)
Hattie Veurink ('42)
David Vila
Cora Vogel ('47)
Rev. Dick H. Walters
Joanne Warners
Dr. J. Dudley Woodberry
Marianne Wrubel
Ronald L. Zoet
Gladys Zuidema ('63)
Mrs. Mary E. Zwaandstra

*Every effort has been made to obtain a complete list of employees over the course of the school's history. Kuyper College regrets any omissions.*

# Appendix C

## 2013-2014 Kuyper College Faculty and Staff

| Name | Title |
|------|-------|
| Jeff Bettig | Food Service Director, Chef |
| John Bills | Computer Support Engineer |
| Alyssa Blom ('13) | Administrative Assistant for Advancement |
| Roger Bouwma | Senior Development Representative |
| Duane Bras | Vice President for Business and Finance |
| Ken Capisciolto | Vice President for College Advancement |
| Mary Carlson | Human Resources |
| Dr. Kai Ton Chau | Associate Professor of Worship Studies, Jack VanLaar Endowed Chair of Music & Worship |
| Tim Chupp ('80) | Supervisor of Maintenance |
| Marc Creviere | Information Technology Director |
| Becki Doornbos | Business Office Assistant |
| Julie Dunning | Enrollment Office Assistant |
| Curt Essenburg ('06) | Director of Student Life |
| Dr. Doug Felch | Professor of Theological Studies |
| Dr. Jeff Fisher | Assistant Professor of Theological Studies |
| Dr. Lisa Garvelink | Professor of English |
| Dr. Patricia R. Harris | Provost |
| Debbie Hendricks | Faculty Associate in Assessment, Instructor of Drama |
| Kirsten Herich | Senior Admissions Counselor and Visit Coordinator |
| Dr. Carol Hochhalter | Associate Professor of Worship Studies |
| Lisa Hoogeboom ('91) | Assistant Professor of Intercultural and Biblical Studies |
| Joel Huizinga ('88) | Custodian |
| Teresa Janzen | Senior Development Representative, Coordinator of Annual Fund |
| Stan Jesky | Men's Basketball Coach |
| Aaron Kenemer | Cross Country Coach |
| Dr. Dan Kroeze ('81) | Professor of Biblical Studies |
| Dr. Nick Kroeze | President |
| Dale Kuiper | Vice President for Enrollment Management |
| Kathy Laarman | Counselor |
| Dawn Lynema | Assistant to the President |

| | |
|---|---|
| Dr. Jessica Maddox | Director of Assessment |
| Dr. Judi Ravenhorst Meerman ('91) | Professor of Social Work, Director of Field Practicum |
| Dr. Ben Meyer | Registrar |
| Christine Moran | Athletic Director, Associate Professor of Physical Education |
| | |
| Luke Morgan | Assistant Director of Admissions and Financial Aid |
| Michelle Norquist | Associate Director of Library Services |
| Kelly Oosterbroek | Wedding Coordinator |
| Dr. Branson Parler | Associate Professor of Theological Studies |
| Jana Postma | Student Life Coordinator |
| Teresa Renkema | Professor of Intercultural Communication |
| Angela Roosma ('12) | Academic Support Associate |
| Eric Roosma ('11) | Director of Facilities and Safety |
| Joshua Rumbarger ('12) | Admissions Counselor |
| Agnes Russell | Director of Financial Aid |
| Hannah R. Schierbeek ('10) | Coordinator for Alumni and Parent Relations |
| Greg Scott | Professor of Social Work, Social Work Program Director |
| Matt Smith | Men's Soccer Coach |
| Chris Steele | Information Technology Associate |
| Carrie Steenwyk | Instructor of English |
| Brenda Swanson | Bookkeeper |
| Rev. Brian Telzerow ('97) | Professor of Youth Ministry |
| Jeff Timmer | Resident Director, Career Services Coordinator |
| Donna K. Vanderkodde ('12) | Assistant to the Registrar |
| Mary VanderMeer | International Student Services Coordinator, Assistant to the Provost |
| | |
| Michelle Walsh | Catering Coordinator, Kitchen Assistant |
| Dr. Richelle White | Associate Professor of Youth Ministry |
| Michael Wiggers | Women's Volleyball Coach |
| Becca Willis | Academic Projects Assistant |
| Michael Wozniak | Athletic Chaplain |
| Dianne Zandbergen ('76) | Director of Library Services |
| Andrew Zwart | Academic Support Coordinator |

# Bibliography

*The Banner*, Christian Reformed Church, 1920-1945.

Bloem, Dan F. "Reformed Bible College: Higher Education for Lay and Mission Workers." *Origins: Historical Magazine of the Archives*, January 2001: 61-66. Print.

Bloem, Dan F. *Reformed Bible College: The Roots and the Fruits*. RBC Ministries, 2003.

*Born in Faith, Nurtured in Prayer*. RBC Ministries, 1989.

DeJong, James A. *Henry J. Kuiper: Shaping the Christian Reformed Church, 1907-1962*. Grand Rapids: William B. Eerdmans Publishing Company, 2007.

*Kuyper College News*, 2006-2014.

*Origins: Historical Magazine of The Archives: Calvin College and Calvin Theological Seminary* Volume XIX Number 1, 2001, pgs. 61-66.

*RBC Lives of Purpose*, 2004-2006.

*Reformed Bible College News Magazine*, 1998-2004.

*Reformed Bible College Newsletter*, 1972-1997.

*Reformed Bible Institute Bulletin*, 1957-1965.

*Reformed Bible Institute Newsletter*, 1965-1971.

*Reformed Bible Institute Quarterly*, 1941-1956.

Veenstra, Johanna. *Pioneering for Christ in the Sudan*. Grand Rapids: Smitter Book Company Publishers, 1926.

KUYPER COLLEGE

# Index

# About the Authors

## Anne Bauman

Anne (Bronkema) Bauman is a copywriter and publicist at RBC Ministries (*Our Daily Bread*) and Discovery House Publishers. She graduated from Kuyper College in 2011 as one of the first four graduates with an English professional studies major along with the standard Bible and theology major. While she was a student at Kuyper, Anne was a teacher's assistant for Dr. Dan Kroeze and Dr. Lisa Garvelink and worked in the Zondervan Library and the Writing Center.

Anne currently enjoys blogging, arts and crafts, and camping. She and her husband Ken live in Grand Rapids.

## Dr. Paul Bremer

Dr. Paul Bremer joined the faculty of Kuyper College (then Reformed Bible College) in 1975. At that time the college was developing its pre-seminary program. He assisted in developing a program of study in philosophy and in New Testament Greek language to serve students who desired to continue their education at a seminary—this resulted in many students from other colleges taking this Greek program, as well.

Paul also served as academic vice president for a number of years. In that role he gave leadership to the college in gaining recognition with the North Central Association and its Higher Learning Commission. As an ordained pastor in the Christian Reformed Church, Paul has done extensive preaching and speaking in Reformed and Presbyterian circles.

Since his retirement from Kuyper in 2006, Paul has pursued his interests in study of Abraham Lincoln and in study of the Navajo Code Talkers of World War II. In 2013, he was the recipient of the Kuyper College H. J. Kuiper Founder's Service Award. Paul and his wife Jacquellyn live in Grand Rapids and have three married children and eleven grandchildren.